K·I·S·S

GUIDE TO

Organizing
Your Life

DONALD E. WETMORE

Foreword by Lenny Laskowski
Acclaimed author and public speaker

A Dorling Kindersley Book

D0010081

LONDON, NEW YORK,
MUNICH, MELBOURNE, DELHI

DK Publishing, Inc.
Editor Lynn R. Northrup
Senior Editor Jennifer Williams
Category Publisher LaVonne Carlson

Dorling Kindersley Limited
Project Editor Caroline Hunt
Managing Editor Maxine Lewis
Managing Art Editor Heather McCarry

Production Heather Hughes
Category Publisher Mary Thompson

Created and produced for Dorling Kindersley by
THE FOUNDRY, part of The Foundry Creative Media Company Ltd,
Crabtree Hall, Crabtree Lane, Fulham, London SW6 6TY

The Foundry project team
Frances Banfield, Jennifer Bishop, Claire Dashwood,
Chris Herbert, Graham Stride, and Polly Willis

Copyright © 2001
DK Publishing, Inc.
Text copyright © 2001 Donald E. Wetmore
001 002 003 004 005 10 9 8 7 6 5 4 3 2

Published in the United States by
DK Publishing, Inc.
375 Hudson Street,
New York, NY 10014

All rights reserved under International and Pan-American Copyright Conventions. No part of this
publication may be reproduced, stored in a retrieval system, or transmitted in any form or by any means,
electronic, mechanical, photocopying, recording, or otherwise, without the prior written permission of
the copyright owner. Published in Great Britain by Dorling Kindersley Limited.

Library of Congress Cataloging-in-Publication Data

Wetmore, Donald E.
     KISS guide to organizing your life / Donald E. Wetmore.
          p. cm. — (Keep it simple series)
          Includes index.
          ISBN 0-7894-8072-7 (alk. paper)
    1. Success.   I. Title. II. Series.
    BJ1611.2 .W44 2001
    646.7—dc21
                                    2001002586
                                       CIP

DK Publishing, Inc. offers special discounts for bulk purchases for sales promotions or premiums.
Specific, large-quantity needs can be met with special editions, including personalized covers,
excerpts of existing guides, and corporate imprints. For more information, contact Special Markets Department,
DK Publishing, Inc., 375 Hudson Street, New York, NY 10014.

Color reproduction by ColourScan, Singapore
Printed and bound by MOHN media and Mohndruck GmbH, Germany

See our complete product line at
www.dk.com

Contents at a Glance

PART ONE

You Can Be In Control

The Basics for Organizing Your Life
Balancing Your Life
The Power of Daily Planning
Managing Those Competing Priorities
Organizing Scheduled Events

PART TWO

Overcoming Barriers and Building Blocks

Crisis Management
Other Useful Tools for
Getting Organized
Overcoming Procrastination
The Importance of Delegation
Specific Ways to Delegate

PART THREE

Getting More Organized

Maximizing Meeting Time
Using a Clean Work Area
Managing Paperwork
The Time Log

PART FOUR

More Timely Tools

Dealing with Interruptions
The Interruptions Log
The Life Improvement Chart
The 7 x 7 Technique
The Personal Productivity System
Practices for Your Personal Life

CONTENTS

Foreword   18
Introduction   20
What's Inside?   22
The Extras   23

PART ONE: You Can Be in Control

CHAPTER 1: The Basics for Organizing Your Life   26

You cannot manage time   28
Productivity: the old definition   31
Productivity: the new definition   34
Step 1: Rate your productivity from 1 to 10   36

CHAPTER 2: *Balancing Your Life* 38

The seven vital areas of your life 40
Pressures that put us out of balance 50
Setting a weekly time budget 52
Having a super day every day 52
Step 2: Complete the balance wheel 54

CHAPTER 3: *The Power of Daily Planning* 56

Why have a daily plan? 58
A tank operator without a general 62
Creating a to-do list 64
Step 3: Make up your to-do list 71

CHAPTER 4: *Managing Those Competing Priorities* 72

Deciding what's crucial and what's not crucial   74
A simple prioritizing system   80
It's a stress reducer   82
Step 4: Prioritize your to-do list   85

CHAPTER 5: *Organizing Scheduled Events* 86

The holistic approach: use one calendar   88
Get a full month at a glance   88
Step 5: Create your calendar of scheduled events 99

PART TWO: Overcoming Barriers and Building Blocks

CHAPTER 6: Crisis Management 102

What is crisis management? 104

Why it happens 106

A tool to fix it: the crisis management log 109

Most crises can be prevented 112

Step 6: Run your crisis management log 113

CHAPTER 7: *Other Useful Tools for Getting Organized* **114**

Using index cards	116
Keep an irritations list	118
Make a gift list	119
Address and phone directory	122
Improving the job each day	125
A portable file cabinet	126
Step 7: Start using these useful tools	127

CHAPTER 8: *Overcoming Procrastination* **128**

Why we procrastinate	130
Pain and pleasure is what motivates us	132
Conquering procrastination	136
Step 8: List your procrastinated items and solutions	143

CHAPTER 9: *The Importance of Delegation*   144

Plugging into someone else's time stream   146
You already delegate a lot   147
The hardest part about delegating   150
Use networking for more results   154
Step 9: Decide what tasks you could
    have delegated to others   157

CHAPTER 10: *Specific Ways to Delegate*   158

Delegating to staff: ask and you may receive   160
Reverse delegation   162
Your inner circle   165
College "gophers"   166
Hiring some extra help   168
Step 10: Decide what and to whom
    you can delegate   169

PART THREE: Getting More Organized

CHAPTER 11: Maximizing Meeting Time   172

Is this meeting necessary?	174
Is your attendance necessary?	176
Create an agenda	179
Assign a time and stick to it	180
Do away with amenities	186
Step 11: Determine which future meetings you can skip	189

CHAPTER 12: *Using a Clean Work Area*   190

If it's out of sight, it's out of mind   192
If it's in sight, it's in mind   194
Our focus goes to the easy and fun stuff   195
Clean it up!   197
Step 12: Schedule a date to clean up
      your work area   201

CHAPTER 13: *Managing Paperwork*   202

Getting off the lists   204
Screening your paperwork   208
Dealing with paperwork   210
Managing e-mails   213
Step 13: Getting a handle on your paperwork   217

CHAPTER 14: *The Time Log*   218

It's like a photo album   220
Using a time log   222
Here's what you'll discover   225
Step 14: Schedule your time log   235

PART FOUR: More Timely Tools

CHAPTER 15: Dealing with Interruptions   238

Life's little unanticipated events   240
Good and bad interruptions   241
Step 15: Keep a log of who you interrupt   251

CHAPTER 16: *The Interruptions Log*   **252**

Creating an interruptions log   254
It's for your eyes only, so be candid   257
What your interruptions log tells you   259
Coworker interruptus   263
Step 16: Keep an interruptions log   267

CHAPTER 17: *The Life Improvement Chart*   **268**

How's your life going?   270
Filling in your life improvement chart   272
Prepare your chart twice a year   280
Step 17: Schedule your life improvement chart   281

CHAPTER 18: *The 7 x 7 Technique*   282

A few improvements each day can
    add up to a lot   284
Making a better tomorrow   285
Acknowledging others   289
What goes around comes around   292
Step 18: List your seven little improvements
    for tomorrow   295

CHAPTER 19: *The Personal Productivity System*   296

The building blocks for increased personal
    productivity   298
Climbing the personal productivity ladder   299
Where are you on the personal productivity
    ladder?   309
Why the Olympians are good role models   313
Step 19: Use the personal productivity
    system each day   315

CHAPTER 20: *Practices for Your Personal Life* 316

Make time for your family and friends   318
Schedule maintenance   323
Job transition tips   326
Continuous personal improvement   329
Step 20: Schedule time for family, maintenance,
        and organizing your home   331

APPENDICES

Organizing your life: the steps   332
To-do lists   336
Further reading   338
Web sites   340
A simple glossary   342
Index   346
Acknowledgments   352

Foreword

AS A PROFESSIONAL SPEAKER *and author of several books on presentation skills and public speaking, I've always had a keen appreciation for the management of time. In fact, I had the privilege of participating in one of Don Wetmore's three-day programs about 10 years ago, and still use his strategies today in my own business. My most recent book,* 10 Days to More Confident Public Speaking *(Warner Books, 2001) would not have been completed on time if I hadn't been well organized. As an international professional speaker, I spend a lot of time traveling and I know from first hand experience that there is a correlation between good time management and career success. The opposite is true as well. Failing to manage your time will limit your opportunities for success.*

Beyond career success, however, managing your time effectively permits you to do more of the things you want to do and enjoy a better quality of life every day – both at work and at home. The K.I.S.S. Guide to Organizing Your Life guides you along the path to more effective time management, starting with the important step of balancing your life. After all, good time management isn't based on doing the wrong things quicker – that just gets you nowhere faster. Instead, this guide shows you how to achieve better balance in every aspect of your life.

Don has taken a complex topic and boiled it down to a simple step-by-step plan that can be readily implemented by all readers – and I like that. There's enough complexity in your life already; the last thing you need is an even more complex and cumbersome system to manage it! Luckily, Don has devised a easy-to-implement, 20-step action plan to organize your life. In fact, if you follow one of Don's steps each weekday for the next four weeks, you will be surprised by the enormous strides you'll make toward managing – and enjoying – tasks and responsibilities that may once have seemed overwhelming.

And who could be a better choice to write about this topic? Don has been a professional speaker on the subject of time management for the last 20 years, and has made over 2,000 presentations to audiences from around the globe. He is a Professional Member of the National Speakers Association and is widely regarded as one the leading experts in the field of time management today. He has authored dozens of published articles on this topic and is frequently interviewed by major media including USA Today, Dallas Morning News, and ABC Radio.

Most important, he walks the talk. The techniques he shares with you in these pages are the tools he uses to manage his own time, both personal and professional. The methods Don writes about, and uses every day, are not lofty theory but, rather, practical, common sense tools and techniques that he has tested himself: They work for him – and they can work for you, too. I have been fortunate to know Don, not only as a colleague, but as a friend.

Enjoy the journey to a better organized life!

Lenny Laskowski

LENNY LASKOWSKI

Introduction

I AM EXCITED FOR YOU! You are about to embark on a journey toward better organization in your life, both at work and at home. Getting organized will help you get more done in less time and with less stress, allowing you more time for the truly important things in your life.

Early on in my adult life I was probably the least likely person to write a book about organizing your life. I was truly the poster boy for poor organization. I resisted any type of structure, such as making up daily to-do lists, for fear that it would take away my spontaneity and restrain me from doing what I wanted to do. I discovered the result was just the opposite. With a little effort, using the simple tools I share with you in these chapters, I was more spontaneous and able to accomplish much more.

It was such a dramatic turnaround in my own personal life that I presented seminars on the topic and taught others these techniques. During the last 20 years, I have made over 2,000 presentations to over 100,000 people from around the globe, all of whom wanted more from their lives.

Organizing your life does not require that you become consumed with the process. You probably have enough complexity in your life. So, if you were to attempt a complex solution to organizing your life, the additional complexity would not serve you well.

The goal of organizing your life is not perfection. None of us will ever be perfectly organized. You are already organized to some degree, otherwise you would not be able to function in this world! Your goal in reading these pages would be to get better organized.

I have written a guide that is simple, fun, and easy to follow. I wanted to provide you with a set of tools that you could readily implement, without hassle or complexity. In each chapter you'll find simple tools and techniques to use immediately.

And the payoff? You will feel more in control, with less stress. You will be able to get the "have to" tasks done more easily, leaving you with a lot more time for the "want to" items. These include spending more time with your family and friends, enjoying hobbies and personal interests, and most of all, just sitting back to enjoy your life more fully.

Donald E. Wetmore

DONALD E. WETMORE

Dedication

This book is dedicated to my wife Nancy and our four marvelous kids, Jennifer, Pamela, Christopher, and Jonathan. Individually and together, they have given me meaning and purpose in my life that no solo traveler could ever have experienced along their life path.

What's Inside?

THE K.I.S.S. GUIDE TO ORGANIZING YOUR LIFE is designed to provide you with simple, fun tools and techniques that you can use right away to help you become better organized, both at work and at home. By applying these tools, you'll be in better control, get more done in less time, and have more time for the things you really want to do.

PART ONE

In Part One I'll show you the importance of maintaining balance and control in your life and provide you with the simple tools to help you to do it. None of us can do everything, but you'll learn how to get the most important things done.

PART TWO

In Part Two I'll show you how to deal with crisis management and procrastination, and I'll tell you about the building blocks that bring you to a higher level of organization and success.

PART THREE

In Part Three I'll help you to get even more organized as you learn the tricks to use to maximize meeting time, work with a clean desk to improve your productivity, and get a handle on paperwork. You'll also learn about the time log, a simple yet powerful tool to help you make small adjustments in your day to leverage your time.

PART FOUR

In Part Four, I'll tell you how to control and manage interruptions that can throw you off your stride, and how the life-improvement chart and the personal productivity system can serve as daily guides to organizing your life. I'll wrap things up with a look at how you can become more organized at home.

The Extras

THROUGHOUT THE BOOK, *you'll find four types of icons scattered. They're meant to act as road signs, drawing your attention to specific types of information. Here are the icons and what they mean:*

Very Important Point

This symbol points out a topic that deserves careful attention. You really need to know this information before continuing.

Complete No-No

This is a warning, something I want to advise you to be aware of or avoid.

Getting Technical

When the information is about to get a bit technical, I'll let you know so that you can read carefully.

Inside Scoop

These are special suggestions and insider tips that will help you reach your goal.

You'll also find some little boxes that include information I think is important, useful, or just plain fun.

Trivia...
These are fascinating facts and little tidbits that give you an insight into all aspects of organizing your life.

DEFINITION
*I'll **define** words and terms that may be unfamiliar to you in an easy-to-understand style. There is a glossary at the back of the book in case you need extra definitions.*

INTERNET
www.internet.com

The Internet is a great source of information and resources for organizing your life, so I've scouted out some of the most interesting web sites for you to check out.

PART ONE

Chapter 1
The Basics for Organizing Your Life

Chapter 2
Balancing Your Life

Chapter 3
The Power of Daily Planning

Chapter 4
Managing Those Competing Priorities

Chapter 5
Organizing Scheduled Events

YOU CAN BE IN CONTROL

W<small>E ALL SEEM TO HAVE</small> too much to do, which says a lot of nice things about us because it means we're entrusted with many *responsibilities*. But this can create stresses that can interfere with our *productivity* as we try to get everything done.

No one can control time, of course. It just goes on and on. What you can control is how you spend your time. After all, if you're not in control, someone or something else probably is, and your time won't be spent the way you would wish it to be. You can easily enjoy more control over each and every day as you become more effective in *organizing your life* by using the 20 simple steps you'll find in this book. Part One will start you on your journey toward becoming more organized!

Chapter 1

The Basics for Organizing Your Life

Time is the great equalizer. We all get the same number of hours each day. Some people are able to organize their lives with consistently high results and successes in many dimensions of their lives while others never seem to be able to accomplish what they want. The purpose of this book is to show you how much more organized you can become to enjoy greater successes throughout your life. You will learn 20 simple steps that will help you get more organized so you can enjoy more success throughout your life – in less time, with less stress!

In this chapter...

✔ You cannot manage time

✔ Productivity: the old definition

✔ Productivity: the new definition

✔ Step 1: Rate your productivity from 1 to 10

You cannot manage time

AS A PROFESSIONAL SPEAKER *for the last 20 years, I have conducted over 2,000 presentations to audiences around the world. I conduct over 150 speaking engagements per year about organizing your life and effective time management. Often, when I begin a presentation, I will say to the audience, "I have been hired to be here with you today to speak about a topic I don't believe in – **time management**." The response is often puzzlement. But then I explain that while no one can really manage time – it just goes on whether you manage it or not – you can manage yourself in relation to time. And that's a big difference.*

> ### DEFINITION
>
> **Time management** *is the art, science, and practice of gaining better control (not absolute control) over the entire 24 hours in your day to create both personal balance and increased productivity.*

Another truth about time is that it can only be spent, it cannot be saved. Did you ever have any time left over at the end of a week that you could move into the next week? Wouldn't that be great if it were possible? But, of course, it's not. And there are only two ways to spend time: wisely or, well, not so wisely.

Did you ever notice that there are some people whom you admire because they seem to be consistent high achievers on a variety of levels? On the other hand, there are some people who just can't get it together. They seem caught up in spinning their wheels without a lot of traction. The difference can't be the quantity of time they have to spend, for we all have the same quantity. Highly successful people from all walks of life achieve more because they use their time differently.

■ **To emulate** *the success of high achievers, give some thought to how you manage your time.*

For example, let's compare two people and their incomes. The first person makes $10,000 per year and the second person makes $100,000 per year. It's not wrong that one makes less than the other. It's just different. Assuming both have the same relative abilities, are of the same age, and have been offered the same opportunities throughout their lives, how do you account for the difference in their income levels? Why does the second person earn ten times what the first person earns? Is it because the second person has ten times more time to earn money? Of course not! The second person makes more money because he or she uses time differently to develop the skills to earn at higher levels.

■ **If you feel** *that you are constantly running from one thing to another, maybe it's time to take control of your time, instead of letting it control of you.*

Do you want more success in your life? Don't spend any more time. Just spend it differently.

Your **personal productivity** is the measurement of what you accomplish in your brief stay on earth, not what you leave undone. You will leave undone far more than you ever get done, accomplishing but a tiny fraction of what you wish do.

DEFINITION

Personal productivity *is the measurement of what you accomplish each day. It includes all our successes throughout the entire 24 hours of every day, in each and every dimension of our lives.*

This is why I get frustrated when I hear someone say, "I'm bored." Now for some children, that's the daily operative phrase: "Oh, that's boring!" But as a grown-up, how can you be bored? There's a big building up the street from you called a library. You can spend a lot of time in there and not be bored. There's another building nearby called a movie theater with several screens and movie offerings. You can spend a lot of time at the movies without being bored. I can understand being frustrated, stressed, and frazzled. But bored? How can any of us be bored in this exciting world?

With all the technological advances of the last couple of decades, you would think we would be getting more done in less time. But for many, the opposite is true. Many people are working longer hours today than a few years ago and have much less leisure time. Couple that with a growing array of choices (500 channels on cable TV, more affluence, and the Internet, just to name a few) and no wonder many people feel stressed! We get more information tossed at us in one day than our great-grandparents typically received in a lifetime. Think about it. In a typical day 100 years ago, you might have browsed through a seed catalog, read your favorite book (and you didn't have many to chose from), and maybe spotted a road sign or two. Today, during almost every waking moment, we are bombarded with information. The radio, TV, Internet, warning labels, and junk mail flood us with information to process at an ever-growing rate.

Trivia...

The average employed person today is working 15 percent more hours than just 10 years ago and has one-third less leisure time. What makes it all the more difficult is that we have significantly more choices today than 10 years ago of how we can spend our time, and, accordingly, we feel significantly more stressed.

■ **Finding enough time** *for leisure and relaxation may seem like a challenge, but you can't achieve a balanced life without it.*

Productivity: the old definition

MANY OF US HAVE been taught definitions about our personal productivity that may no longer be as effective in this new millennium – the Information Age – as in years gone by. Let's take a closer look at some of these outmoded definitions.

Working hard

We have been taught for generations to work hard and to get it all done. It began hundreds of years ago with those working the land, which was the majority of the population. If you were a farmer who worked the land, you worked hard because your livelihood depended on it. The harder you worked, the more you accomplished. And so, people were taught to equate working hard with success. Then some farmers moved off the farms to the factories in town where "working hard" was still a fair measure of their success, because the harder you worked at the factory, the greater your output and thus the

■ **Hundreds of years** *of farming set the precedent for equating hard work with success. This is true today, even in our "technological" age.*

potential for personal rewards. During the Industrial Revolution many machines and devices were invented that helped lighten the load, but hard work was still considered the formula for success.

■ **Different careers** *demand different skills, but most people agree that it takes a high level of commitment to achieve our goals, no matter what the job.*

During these simpler times we had fewer responsibilities and fewer choices. Then along came the post-World War II economic expansion that multiplied our responsibilities, choices, and stress levels. With that came much higher expectations and demands on each of us, along with a shift from trading tangible items, such as crops and manufactured goods for wealth creation, to trading information like computer software and data as a basis for wealth creation. How we define personal productivity has changed over the years.

Don't count on yesterday's solutions for today's problems.

■ **The age of the computer** *has brought many new opportunities – and problems – to the workplace.*

■ **The growth of a competitive global marketplace**, *together with longer working hours, is putting more pressure on people to perform at consistently higher levels.*

Economic change

The Information Age will no doubt prove to be a more productive and efficient wealth creator than all previous economic practices for this reason. It feeds off itself and multiplies itself, unlike hard, tangible items. For example, if persons A and B each have $1 (or something worth $1), then between them they have $2 of total value. If A gives his dollar to B, A has nothing and B has $2. If B gives her dollar to A, B has nothing and A has $2. But if A has an idea to improve something and B has a different but equally valuable idea to improve something, together they control two ideas. What if A shares his idea with B and B shares her idea with A? Each still retains the original idea and now has a second idea from the other. What a productivity boon! Unlike most other assets, combining information multiplies itself.

■ **Working all the time** *to "get ahead of the game" does not necessarily bring happiness – many people feel they are under too much pressure to succeed.*

Winning the rat race

My neighbor sports this bumper sticker: "Life's a rat race and the rats are winning." Many people feel that they have too much to do and not enough time to do it. They feel like they cannot work any harder, yet they are still not getting it all done. They may indeed feel like the "rats" (stress, frustration, and reduced productivity) are winning. Many people work more hours today and have fewer leisure hours than 10 years ago because they have been taught to respond to a time management challenge by putting in more time. This would be a worthwhile solution if we had unlimited amounts of time, but we don't.

Productivity: the new definition

I WORK HARD. Most people do, and I am sure you do too. I respect that work ethic of putting in an honest day's work for an honest day's pay. But as most of us have too much to do already and a future that will give us even more responsibilities and choices, we need a new definition for organizing and managing our lives.

Working smart

Here is the starting point of **working smart**. Say to yourself, "I cannot get it all done, but I can get the most important things done." Does that make sense? Your life is much like a sandy beach. Take one grain of sand in the palm of your hand and let that represent everything you have and will accomplish in your life. Then all the other billions of grains of sand around that one grain are the things you could have done. You could have read a chapter in a book last night. You could have gone out for a pizza at lunch today. You could have watched a different television program last weekend. While you could have lots of alternative things, you did what you did.

> **DEFINITION**
>
> **Working smart** *is the practice of leveraging your time for maximum results. It is the understanding that those who achieve greater results in life are not spending any more time, but are using their time differently.*

At our funeral, our friends and loved ones will not be talking about what we could have done in our lives. Rather, they will be remembering us for what we did do and for our achievements. (And hopefully these are positive remembrances and a lot of them!)

■ **Realising that** *you can't "have it all" may be the most effective way to achieve real success, both on a professional and personal level.*

Expensing vs. investing time

Most people are pretty good about managing their money. We spend or "expense" a lot of what we make on items such as food, theater tickets, or magazines. Except for some memories, the value is gone after consuming what we purchased. We also "invest" some of our earnings for things like retirement and a cushion for a rainy day. If we fail to invest some of it our golden years may not be too golden.

■ **Why not learn** *a new skill with your partner or a friend? It'll enrich your life in surprising ways.*

Time is a more precious resource than money because, for most of us, our money comes from the way we use our time. (If you spend all your time locked in your bedroom with the shades pulled down and the covers pulled up over your head, you do not make money. You advance by getting out in the world, learning, and developing relationships and skills.)

Since time is a more precious resource than money, let's think about allocating your time between "expense" and "investment." You "expense" a lot of your time. When you go to a restaurant, shoot the breeze with a coworker, or watch your favorite TV show, you are generally expensing your time. Except for perhaps some memories, you get little back in the future for that time spent. However, when you earn a college degree, develop a new skill such as speed-reading, or create a work of art, you are "investing" your time because it can yield future rewards.

There is an important correlation between investing your time and your successes in life. The more you invest your time, the less you "expense" it, and the greater the results you will enjoy. Want more results in your future? Invest more of your time now.

INTERNET

www.balancetime.com

This time management supersite provides free articles and tips to help you to work smarter and better manage your time with less stress. Articles are updated regularly and there is an online stress test you can take.

An excellent way to increase your future results is to invest a little of your time each day reading one of the chapters in this book. It has been designed as a personal step-by-step course to help you better organize your day in less than a month. Each step builds on the last, helping you to climb higher each day. There are four parts with five chapters in each part, for a total of 20 chapters. Complete a chapter a day, 5 days a week, and in 20 days you will be attaining more results in less time with your new lifetime skills!

Try to set aside the same time each day to complete that day's step – perhaps during your lunch hour, at the beginning of your workday, or at the end of the day instead of watching TV. Or go at your own pace and proceed more rapidly or more slowly. Either way, be sure to take some time to practice what you've just learned. Enjoy the journey and enjoy your results!

Let's start with Step 1.

■ **Once you've started** *learning how to better organize your life, why not share your new-found knowledge with others.*

STEP 1:
RATE YOUR PRODUCTIVITY FROM 1 TO 10

As we quantify certain things it may help us to understand them better. On a scale of 1 to 10, rate your productivity: 1 means "lousy," you don't get anything done; while 10 means "perfect," your productivity could not be any better. Don't rate yourself in just the work environment; take into account your productivity throughout the entire day.

So what's your score? 5? 6? 8? 2? Don't worry if you gave yourself a low score. After all, that's why you're reading this book, right? There is no "right" or "wrong" score. Everyone is unique and cannot be (or should not be) at the same level of productivity. However, most would agree that the lower the number, the lower the productivity;

■ **Start by assessing** *all aspects of your work. It may seem like a daunting task at first, but the payoff over the long term is worth it!*

■ **In today's hectic world**, *it is vital to take control of how you manage your time.*

the higher the number, the higher the productivity. And most would also agree that more productivity is better than less because the more productive you are, the greater the success and rewards you will enjoy.

So whatever your number, ask yourself: What is keeping you from being at a higher number? What would you change if you could to permit you to get to that higher level? Would fewer interruptions in your day make a difference? How about having a staff person or two to help you out? Would you be able to focus better and get more done if your stress level was reduced and you felt more in control?

Make up your list of things that you feel keep you from being at a higher number and look for a solution to every item on your list as you proceed through these chapters.

A simple summary

✓ You cannot manage time, but you can manage how you use your time.

✓ The old definition of productivity, working hard, was a useful measure of success in the past but is less so today.

✓ The new definition of productivity and organizing your life is working smart and leveraging that scarce resource of time for maximum results.

✓ Step 1 for organizing your life is to rate your level of productivity on a scale of 1 to 10.

Chapter 2

Balancing Your Life

ORGANIZING YOUR LIFE EFFECTIVELY has a lot to do with not only what you are doing each day, but also what you may not be doing. You can have the best organizational tools and the greatest plans, but if you are out of balance in your life to begin with, you face the potential of sabotaging your success. Balance is needed in all of life's seven vital areas. Like a seven-legged table, if one leg is longer or shorter than the rest, it will throw the entire table off balance. So it is with our lives. You need to maintain a good daily balance as a foundation for organizing your life.

In this chapter...

✔ The seven vital areas of your life

✔ Pressures that put us out of balance

✔ Setting a weekly time budget

✔ Having a super day every day

✔ Step 2: Complete the balance wheel

AIM TO BE CONTENT IN ALL AREAS OF YOUR LIFE, AS ANY IMBALANCE WILL AFFECT YOUR WELL-BEING

The seven vital areas of your life

YOUR LIFE IS MORE *than just making a living or being a great parent. We all have seven dimensions or vital areas to our lives: health, family, financial, intellectual, social, professional, and spiritual. You may treat your social life differently than your neighbor does, or you may spend more time on your financial affairs than your best friend does. We each select the emphasis we place on each of our seven areas. But we all have a social life, a financial life, and so on.*

DEFINITION

Balance *is maintaining a level of success to your own personal satisfaction in each of your seven vital areas.*

If all the legs on that peculiar seven-legged table are exactly the same length, then that table will be solid. But if we make any one leg (never mind two or three or more) a little longer or shorter than the rest, we upset the stability of the entire table. And so it is with your life. While you won't spend equal amounts of time in each of life's seven vital areas, if, in the long run, you are spending a sufficient quantity and quality of time in each area, your life will be in *balance*.

But look what happens if we get out of balance in just one area, never mind two or three! Let's say you don't have time for health and fitness. You're all tired out from lack of sleep dragging through each day at a low energy level. Your resistance level is low, making you susceptible to all the latest colds and flu bugs going around. Does that interfere with your ability to be the good family person you want to be? Sure it does. Does that interfere with your ability to focus clearly on your professional responsibilities? I'll bet it does.

■ **Keep your life** *in perspective. While getting a big promotion at work may seem more important than anything else, there are other parts of your life that are just as important.*

Let's say things are not going well in your family area. Does that interfere with your spiritual health? Your social life? Do you see how being off balance in one area affects other areas of your life?

The notion of organizing your life is more than just making up a list of things to do for the next day. Organizing your life is about gaining more control over every hour in every day, because if you are not in balance as a starting point, you can't enjoy increased productivity in all areas of your life.

■ **If you are not** *happy in your family area, the effect that this has on you may have a knock-on effect on your work, which in turn could have repercussions on other areas of your life.*

Achieving balance in your life is not a reward once you become successful. It is a necessary ingredient to ensure that you do become successful.

Now it's time for me share a few words with you on the importance of each of these seven areas:

1) Health: extending your life is a choice

This is the area that many people take for granted until they don't have it anymore. Most would be willing to pay anything on the last day of their lives to buy a few more years of quality living. The problem is that no one is going to be there with us on that day to make the sale to us.

I am always intrigued by how carefully people treat their new cars. They bring the car in for the scheduled maintenance, clean it frequently with a nice soft cloth, and always fill the tank with the highest grade of gasoline. If you do all that, the car will last longer; if you don't, the car will wear out a lot quicker. Now I'm not for wearing your new car out too quickly, but the truth is, if you drive it into the ground and don't take care of it, you can always get another one, true? If you have purchased one new car in your life, you have proven your ability to purchase new cars. If you have purchased one, you can purchase two. But if you wear out your body too soon, where are you going to live?

Many deaths are preventable and are caused by what we are doing to ourselves or failing to do for ourselves. If organizing your life has any meaning at all, it means doing things now that will help add years to your life. That means quitting smoking, getting regular checkups, finding more time for exercise, and eating fewer cheeseburgers and fries and more fruit and vegetables.

■ **Take up a new sport** – *and take control of your health. Finding time for regular exercise will enhance the quality of your life.*

Take time for health and fitness today, or you may have to take time for sickness and illness tomorrow.

■ **Food is one of life's** *great pleasures. Eat healthfully and live long!*

2) Family: taking more time for loved ones

According to statistics, roughly half of all marriages today end in divorce. And the number one cause of divorce? A lack of communication. Studies tell us that the average working person spends less than 2 minutes per day in meaningful communication with a spouse or significant other. I don't know about you, but I can't get my story out in 2 minutes per day let alone hear about what my wife did in her day!

Most people I speak with wish they had more time for family. My wife and I raised our four children during our 30-plus years of marriage. We spent a lot of time with each other and our kids because we took the time to do it. We scheduled it. There is only one way to get time. You have to take the time. We all have too much to do and therefore will never get it all done. And while there is never enough time for everything, there is always enough time for the important things like helping your kids with their homework or throwing a ball around, or taking your spouse or partner out to lunch.

■ **Spending time with** *the people you care about is not just enjoyable in itself, it has a positive effect on keeping your life in balance.*

3) Financial: improving your cash flow

We all appreciate the things that money can buy. Here's an area of your life that takes up a huge chunk of your time. As I mentioned in Chapter 1, everyone has 24 hours each day, 7 days each week. That totals 168 hours in the week. No more, no less. Now deduct 56 hours per week for sleep (8 hours a night, 7 nights a week), which might be high for some and low for others. You're left with 112 hours.

■ **Don't assume that** *you'll be more successful than your colleagues just because you put in more hours of work. You may need to spend your time differently, rather than spending more of it, in order to achieve your goals.*

Then you need to subtract the time the average person spends at work, approximately 40 hours per week. (You may work more or fewer hours.) Add another 10 hours for preparation time and commuting time. Therefore, if you are working 45 hours per week, adding 10 hours, it is taking you 55 hours to advance yourself through this world financially. If we subtract 55 hours from 112 hours, we are now left with just 57 hours to do everything else we need to do each week, including eating!

Yet, I have learned that there is very little correlation between the number of hours we work and the financial results we receive. I am not suggesting there is no correlation. Certainly, if you spend no time you are likely to earn no money. Those who enjoy mega-incomes are often very talented and occasionally very lucky people. Some may be smarter than the average person. What they don't have is more time than anyone else. The secret then? They use their time differently. They may delegate some responsibilities to others, or prioritize their work so the most important tasks get done first.

■ **Watch how the** *most efficient of your colleagues manage their time. As busy as they are, you may be surprised by how much extra time they have.*

Earning levels in this world range from zero (if you do nothing) to billions. Yet those who make significantly more than the average person have no more time than anyone else. Do you want more money? Use your time differently – don't spend any more of it.

4) Intellectual: continuing to learn

What we know – our ability to think and reason – is what separates human beings from the rest of the animal kingdom. And if you think about it, most of what you have going for you now in each of your seven vital areas has come to you through a lifetime of learning. We all come into this world the same way, broke and naked. And we all leave the same way, broke (they give us some clothes).

When you were born, you didn't know how to drink from a cup, punch a computer key, read a good book about organizing your life, or drive a standard-shift car. (Okay, maybe you're still having trouble mastering a standard-shift car!) But you learned these things as you progressed through your life.

The old rules said that as you came into your working years you learned a skill, trade, or profession. This knowledge qualified you for the plateau of employment. For the rest of your working life, you could pretty much rely on the talents you acquired as a young person. Sure, you would learn and get better at what you did, but you relied heavily on the skill set developed early on. Little changed, including your skill level, as the years passed by.

I am going to make a prediction: If you continue doing what you do today, without change or improvement, there is a high probability that you could be obsolete in your job within the next five years or so. Do you agree? Pretty scary, huh? It's scary because we all like our comfort zones. We like doing things the way we have always done things. But in this new Information Age, knowledge is power, and we can no longer afford to linger in that comfort zone. The only way to broaden your horizons is to take the time to do it. I budget one training day per month to attend workshops and seminars that will help my professional speaking business.

If you commute to work each day, use that time productively to stay ahead of the curve. There is a wide selection of audiotapes out there at your local bookstore or library on almost any topic you can imagine. There are tapes on sharpening your management skills, becoming a better parent, and learning a foreign language, just to name a few; as well as the latest bestsellers on tape.

■ **Put your half-hour** *commute to valuable use: invest in an audio course, and a whole new world of opportunity could open up to you.*

Listen to those audiotapes during the commute to work (being careful to keep your eyes on the road, of course). Even a 15-minute commute will produce enormous results over a year. Fifteen minutes twice a day for 5 days is 2½ hours per week, or approximately 125 hours over a year. The average undergraduate college course is approximately 35 classroom hours. Fifteen minutes a day of selected audiotape listening is the rough equivalent of three or four college courses per year. You now have your own University on Wheels!

The average person reads approximately 200 words per minute for 2 hours per day. If you could double your reading speed you could cut your reading time in half, or read for the same amount of time but twice as much. If this sounds good, consider enrolling in a speed-reading class.

Did you know that you can become recognized as a world-class expert in a topic of your choice in as little as 3 to 5 years by taking just one hour of focused "me time" study per day? Would your future be more profitable, enjoyable, less stressful, and enriched if you did this? One hour a day, 365 hours per year. If the average college class is 35 classroom hours, that's the rough equivalent of ten college courses per year. You are a full-time student!

■ **Enroll in a day course** *or weekly class that relates to your area of expertise. It will enrich both your professional and personal life.*

■ **You may be surprised** *to discover where you can "find" the time to learn a foreign language or research a new career-try shaving a few hours off the time you spend watching TV.*

In the next 3 to 5 years you can master a foreign language, write a great book, develop and become expert at a new hobby, develop your own part-time business or investment program, or whatever is of interest to you.

Where do you find that hour each day? You take it. Schedule it. Make different choices and use your time differently. Perhaps you can get up an hour earlier or stay up an hour later, or cut away an hour of television. If you set your mind to it, you will find that extra hour. Why? Because it was always there in disguise; you were just using it for something else.

5) Social: making time for friends

I think most people value a good social life. If that were not true, most people would be hermits living alone in the woods somewhere. A rich social life with real friends adds a true dimension of quality to our lives.

■ **Make new ones**, *meet up with old ones; whatever you do, make time for friendship in your life – no one can ever have enough friends.*

Ever wonder why some people have so many friends and others so few? It comes down to choices. The person with many friends has chosen to use his or her time in such a way as to create a full social life. The person with few friends has made different choices – not wrong choices, just different ones.

So how do you make a friend? One at a time. There are over six billion people on our planet. Take your pick as to who you would like to be friends with. It takes time and effort – to have a friend you must be a friend. Schedule the time to be with your friends and make time to meet new ones. Join a club, take a class, get involved in a new sport or hobby, volunteer at the local Humane Society . . . your options for meeting people are endless, and you'll be having fun and helping others in the process.

> ### Trivia...
> *If you think of some of the most successful people you admire, they are almost always in balance. This practice is what helped them to become successful in the first place and to stay successful as well.*

6) Professional: achieving inner satisfaction

The professional area is a bit different than the financial area, although what you do for financial reasons you do for professional reasons as well.

What if I told you that starting next week, you had a new job and the job description was to sit at a desk all day long? That's it. That's the entire job. You could not talk to anyone, use a computer, or so much as handle a piece of paper. You just had to sit with your arms folded all day long and stare at a wall. You would receive the same paycheck and benefits as any other job. Do you see the difference between that and a job you enjoy? Sure, the money part of employment is important, but what about that feeling of satisfaction you get from your work? We all need to enjoy that inner satisfaction that comes from knowing we did a good job, that we made a difference, and put some footprints in the ground out there. That's what the professional area is all about.

■ **Although everyone** *gets different things out of what they do to earn a living, most of us want the satisfaction of doing a job to the best of our ability.*

7) Spiritual: living true to your heart

While more than 80 percent of us practice a formal religion, the spiritual area is not just religion. It may include our religious practice plus our relationships to one another, to our communities, and to our environment. It is the area that adds meaning and purpose to our lives as we extend our efforts beyond our own purposes toward the benefit of others.

You can receive enormous satisfaction practicing random acts of kindness through volunteer work, charitable donations, or just giving someone a helping hand. You make a better community for everyone as well.

INTERNET

www.topica.com/lists/ timemanagement

This site offers free "Timely Time Management Tips" on a regular basis to help you increase your personal productivity.

■ **Help fix your friend's car**, *pick up a neighbor's groceries, help out a charity store, read stories to the kids at the local elementary school: make a difference to someone's life!*

Pressures that put us out of balance

IT'S EASY TO GET thrown out of balance in the seven vital areas of life. Why? Because almost everyone you encounter has a different idea about how you should spend your time. Your family will take all your time if you let them. Your job will take all of your time if you let it. So will your friends. This doesn't make any of these people or things bad, it's just the way the world works.

If there is a void in your time management and organizational life, someone or something will step in to fill it and lead you. The problem is that they may not play out your time in a way that is going to create balance and happiness in your life.

■ If your life *is in balance, the obstacles you once thought of as insurmountable will appear far less daunting, but if it is not, then often the smallest irritations or worries can become blown out of all proportion.*

Almost over the hump

You may be saying, "Right now I've got so much to do, I can't afford to be in balance. Just as soon as I get over the hump, then I'll have the time to create this balance you write about." The problem is, as soon as you are over your current hump, there will be another hump or challenge you will have to contend with. Isn't that true? Has there ever been a time in your life when you did not have humps or challenges?

Creating balance is not a reward for becoming successful. It is a necessary building block, because without being in balance in the first place, you are often sabotaging your success.

■ **Every aspect** *of your life is as important as the other: don't assume that by keeping yourself healthy your financial affairs will be sorted out.*

Uni- and duo-dimensional

A stool requires at least three legs to remain standing. Let's say you build your life on only one or two of the seven vital areas. You are great at the financial and professional areas, but spend little of your time on the health, family, intellectual, social, and spiritual areas. You become uni- or duo-dimensional.

Don't base your life on just a few "legs" — it places you in a position of unnecessarily high risk of collapse if one or two of those legs are removed. Build your life on a solid base of seven legs. Remember, a stool requires a minimum of three legs to stand up.

And while you are achieving great short-term success, if you are building your life on just one or two legs, what happens if those legs are taken away? It can happen. Your money can disappear overnight. You can lose your job, and your career can vanish in short order. While you can take some precautions to prevent this from happening, the truth is, if one or more legs are taken from you, if your life is in balance you have several others to support you as you go on and rebuild.

■ **The different** *facets of your life make it whole. If you don't take the time to vary your interests and activities you may be sabotaging your own efforts to achieve a balanced life.*

Setting a weekly time budget

MANY PEOPLE USE *a financial budget to allocate the limited resource of money. This way they can maximize what they have to work with. Because time is a more precious asset than money, how about establishing a time budget? It's easy to set up a time budget for the coming week for each of your seven vital areas. For health, for example, ask yourself, "At the end of next week, will I be satisfied having spent no time in the health area?" Of course not. Then ask yourself how much time you would be satisfied with – seven hours? 14 hours? Once you have determined the amount, schedule it to make it happen!*

How much time would you like to say you spent in your family area at the end of the week? None? Twenty hours? You select the answer that makes sense to you and then schedule time for each vital area.

■ **Time is** *like money in the bank: The more you waste the less you have. To make the most of your time, always think carefully about how to spend it.*

Having a super day every day

IMAGINE GOING TO BED *tonight and as your head hits the pillow, taking an inventory of the seven vital areas, rating your performance in each area today on a scale of 1 to 10 (1 being "lousy" and 10 being "perfect"). And let's say that in this one day, every one of the areas was a 10 in your opinion.*

You were busy today, but you squeezed out time to go to the gym. You managed to get some time helping your daughter with her homework. You set up an appointment with a financial manager, something you've been meaning to do for some time. You found about 45 minutes to do some of that independent reading you've been intending to do. You had lunch with friends. You got a lot done at work, and even found time to take a peaceful walk in the park.

■ **Spending time** *with loved ones will not only benefit them, it will also give you a sense of wellbeing, especially if your experiences at work have been less than ideal.*

Sure, the day wasn't without problems and aggravations. Maybe someone cut you off in traffic, or was rude to you over the phone. A coworker might have said an unkind thing to you, or an expected package didn't arrive in the mail. But when your life is in balance, it can still be a super day!

If you are having a rough ride down the road of life, it may have more to do with your wheels than the road. The road may be perfect, but if your wheels are not, your ride will be bumpy.

■ **Once you find** *that you can make time for the things you really like to do, such as walking your dog, rather than just the things you have to do, you may find you are more motivated to get your life into focus.*

STEP 2:
COMPLETE THE BALANCE WHEEL

Rate your current performance, as of this day, in each of your seven vital areas on the following balance wheel, from 1 ("lousy") to ten ("perfect"). It's a good idea to make several copies of this chart before you fill it in so you can use it for other days too.

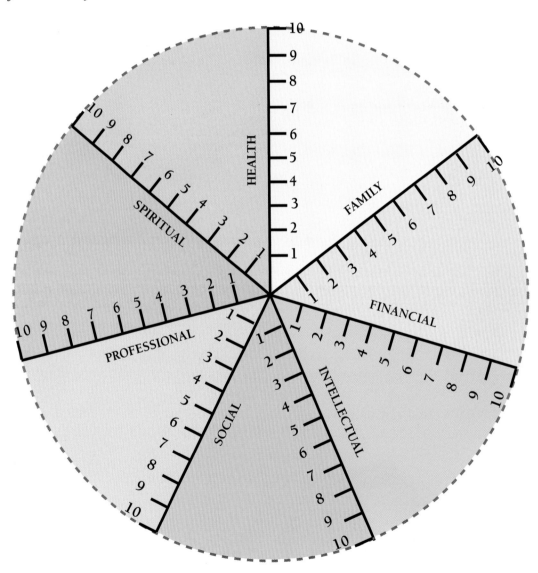

After you have practiced the rest of the steps in this book, rate yourself again and see if the areas in your wheel have become a bit more balanced, giving you a smoother ride down the road of life.

■ **A good balance** *in life can only be achieved once you have realised that to get there takes some effort – and that you have to work on all areas of your life.*

A simple summary

✔ Organizing your life effectively starts with balancing your seven vital areas: health, family, financial, intellectual, social, professional, and spiritual.

✔ Pressures that put us out of balance are all around us. We need to maintain control of our time.

✔ Like a good financial budget, a weekly time budget will maximize the value of the limited time you have each week.

✔ When your seven vital areas are in balance, you can have a super day every day!

✔ Step 2 for organizing your life is to rate your day's performance on the balance wheel.

Chapter 3

The Power of Daily Planning

EACH OF US IS THE PRESIDENT and sole stockholder of a major corporation, Me, Inc. You have sales, expenses, and, hopefully, a profit at the end of year. What if you were to operate without the board of directors concept? Like any organization, you would be pulled in a variety of directions; although you might be working hard, you would actually be accomplishing less than you might otherwise get done. Daily planning is like having a regular board of directors meeting for the most important corporation of all, Me, Inc., so that all the resources at your command over the next 24 hours are all pulling in the same direction, leveraging your time, and maximizing your results.

In this chapter...

✓ Why have a daily plan?

✓ A tank operator without a general

✓ Creating a to-do list

✓ Step 3: Make up your to-do list

TAKE THE BOARD-MEETING APPROACH TO ORGANIZING YOUR LIFE – YOU'LL BE AMAZED AT THE DIFFERENCE

Why have a daily plan?

DAILY PLANNING *is the time you set aside each day to take control over the most precious resource under your control: the next 24 hours. It is said that many people do not plan to fail, but a lot of people do fail to plan. They get dressed, fight the rush-hour traffic, show up where they need to be, and deal with one event after another that's tossed in their direction. This continues throughout their day. At the end of the day they go home, often exhausted. They get some sleep, get up the next morning, throw on a new set of clothes, and repeat the same cycle.*

> **DEFINITION**
>
> **Living life on purpose** *means taking actions consistent with your master plan for your life. It requires taking care of both the things you have to do and want to do.*

That to me is living life by accident. I want you to start *living life on purpose*.

■ **Rather than just hurtling** *head-first into your day without stopping to think what you want to achieve by the end of it, try to give it some structure by making a few well-laid plans first.*

■ **If you feel as if life** *is a constant struggle, it's time to give yourself – and your life – a sense of purpose.*

The daily grind

Let's imagine for a moment that you and nine others work for my fictitious company, The Sled-Moving Corporation. Each day we all put on the leather reins that are attached to a sled and we pull the sled. The purpose of the company is to move this sled as far as possible each day in the direction of north. (This is a kind of a silly company for sure!)

The only problem we have is that we have not been told where north is. Some think north is to the left of where we are. Others feel it is to the right. All of us believe in the notion of putting in a good day's work for a good day's pay. So as we struggle to move the sled, we work against one another, at cross-purposes. At the end of the day, we go home, having moved the sled very little, perhaps only a few yards.

At home that evening, during dinner your partner asks, "Did you have a productive day?" "Of course," you reply. "Pass the potatoes, please." A bit later, your son asks, "How do you know you had a productive day?" "Because," you proudly state, "I worked hard. May I have the bread, please?" This is what you and I have been taught, to equate hard work with productivity. The harder you work, the more productive you must therefore be.

Later during dinner, your daughter asks, "Well, how do you know you worked hard?" Almost indignant, you open your shirt a bit to show the red marks left by the strain of the leather reins against your shoulders from pulling that sled all day. "There, see the marks? This is why I know I worked hard today! The marks prove that I worked hard today. Pass the peas, please."

After dinner, while watching a rerun of your favorite TV show, your partner asks, "How far did the sled move today, dear?" You reply, "Well, it didn't move very far at all today, but I can't wait to get back there tomorrow and do it all over again."

There is a difference between business and busy-ness. Business is doing the things that advance our success. Activity does not necessarily mean productivity.

Knowledge is power

But what if all of us as employees of this sled-moving company can agree that north is in the same direction? In less effort and time than it took to move the sled very little yesterday, we could have that sled half-way across town!

Do you understand that over the next 24 hours, you have enormous resources at your disposal? You have your smarts, your wits, your knowledge, and your charming personality. In addition, you have access to physical assets that you own or others allow you to use. You can access the daily news, the Internet, and the public library. The list is almost endless.

■ **A couple of hours** *of research or a few minutes spent assessing a problem can have a huge pay-off.*

Aiming for a goal

If you don't have a plan for your next 24 hours that identifies north in your life, do you see where some of these resources may be working at cross-purposes, limiting your productivity? This is because many will make demands on your time each day without understanding what your final destination is. However, if you can identify the true direction of your life for the next 24 hours, then you can pull together all the resources at your command in the same direction, magnifying your organizational skills and your productivity.

■ **You will feel** *so much more positive and purposeful if you have something to aim for during the day, so decide on the direction you want to take – and stick to it.*

Your mind is a powerful device. Each person's brain is more powerful than the most powerful computer ever created. This brain of yours is best used to focus on the big picture and not get cluttered with all the details. Sure, the details are important, because they help us to see the big picture. But rather than cluttering up your brain with all the details, write them down on the **to-do list** you prepare each night as part of your daily planning.

DEFINITION

*A **to-do list** is a written list of what you have to do and what you want to do over the next 24 hours. It is your roadmap for the next 24 hours to maximize your success.*

An old Asian maxim suggests that the faintest ink has more power than the strongest mind. In other words, using a weak pen is better than using that magnificent computer in your head. Get it down on paper!

A tank operator without a general

IMAGINE OVERLOOKING A BATTLE SCENE *where you see two important activities going on. First there is a tank operator. It is his job to go to battle each day and shoot at targets. Next is the general whose job is to decide where all the tanks go the next day. Which of these two functions is most important? The tank operator or the general? The general, of course. You might be the best tank operator on the line, able to get out there every day and shoot more rounds of ammunition at more targets than anyone else on the line. But if you're not shooting at targets that have any strategic value, your day is wasted. The general decides in advance where the tanks ought to go the next day and thereby increases their effectiveness and productivity.*

Trivia...

Years ago, battles were fought with each warrior deciding how to spend his energy on the battlefield. It was chaos. It was wasteful. Life is not a war, but we do need a battle plan of sorts to organize our days as we compete with multiple forces for our time.

■ **No one would** *think of sending a tank into battle without a plan, so why should you start your day without a sense of direction?*

There are a lot of people who run their days like a tank operator without a general. I want you to be a general. And there's a war out there, because the truth is, either you are in control of your time, or someone or something else is. Now words like tank operators, generals, and wars all have generally negative connotations, and I am very positive about our topic, as you might already suspect. I use these examples only to make the point. It is the general who knows the master plan, sees the big picture, and can direct the elements within his or her control towards achieving that plan. You must be that general.

But where's the spontaneity?

My wife teases me sometimes about the daily planner I carry around wherever I go. She'll say, "You can't do anything without writing it down in that book!" I understand her teasing, especially after 30 years, but it really is not the case that I have lost my spontaneity.

Many resist doing daily planning for fear that they will sacrifice spontaneity, that they will be locked into doing things. Years ago, I would rarely plan my day. I took things as they happened and hoped for the best. I wanted to be flexible and spontaneous. The problem was, the reverse happened. How would I be spending my tomorrow? I had no idea. It all depended on who was barking the loudest for my attention. I was like a leaf blowing in the wind. My direction was propelled by the biggest gusts that came at me in any given day.

■ **No matter what** *anyone else may say, nothing can beat a daily schedule for giving focus and structure to your day.*

Breaking away from the constraints

Daily planning gets us away from the constraints caused by no planning by taking control of the two dimensions to our next day. When we have committed to do something at a specific date and time we refer to that as an appointment (or a scheduled event). For example, a staff meeting next Tuesday at 10 a.m., a dentist appointment Saturday at 9 a.m., or going to a party this Friday at 7:30 p.m. are all appointments or scheduled events. Everything else we have to and want to do in our day – wash the car, work on a business report, return phone calls, pay bills – are discretionary items, things you do at your discretion around appointments and scheduled events. I'll tell you more about how to effectively manage appointments and scheduled events in Chapter 5. Here, let's discuss how to manage those discretionary items.

Creating a to-do list

YOU CAN CREATE your to-do list on a simple pad of paper or any one of the dozens of more elaborate systems that are available at your local office supply store. I prefer to use a Day-Timer, which is a simple but powerful tool to create your to-do lists and manage your schedules for both business and personal items.

■ **You can structure** *your day down to the last nanosecond, using a personal organizer, or simply make a list – the main thing is to find what works best for you.*

The Day-Timer

I have no financial stake in the Day-Timer, company and make no money if you order products from them. I have been a happy customer of theirs for many years and have found their products to be most useful in organizing my life.

■ **Using a personal organizer** *means that you will never have to worry about losing bits of paper, or search desperately for a pen at that crucial moment – all the information you need is right in the palm of your hand.*

WHY USE A DAY-TIMER?

There are three chief benefits of the Day-Timer systems, or whatever organizational tool you may wish to use:

(1) They offer a holistic system of managing your time that lets you put business and personal to-do items in one single source so you don't have to keep multiple diaries.

(2) They are simple to use.

(3) They are compact enough to carry with you all the time. Some tools are big and cumbersome or attached to a personal computer. These work just fine, but if you can't carry the tool with you, you can't use it effectively.

■ **When you are going** *to be out of the office, make sure that you transfer all the information you need from your day-to-day system to your organizer.*

■ **Despite the number** *of technological advances in computerized personal organizers, many people still prefer – and find it just as convenient – to use pen and paper.*

Handheld electronic tools such as Palm Pilots are becoming increasingly popular. They are trendy and fun to use. But having talked with hundreds of people who have used these electronic systems and compared them with paper systems, the paper system wins out about 80 percent of the time. Much of that is due to old habits or our innate distrust of electronic devices. Time will perfect those devices and no doubt, one day, we will all have a universal appliance that helps us to manage our time and stay in contact with one another.

The bottom line is for you to select a tool to help with your daily planning that you like using and that offers the three benefits I mentioned earlier. Your success in better organizing your life has little to do with the specific tool you select to help you, but rather, the application of the principles I share in these chapters.

Whatever tool you select to help with your daily planning, make sure you feel comfortable using it. If it sits in a drawer and you never use it, what's the point?

The have tos and the want tos

Organizing your life is more than just doing a good job of taking care of the "have-to" items in your life. Sure, the have tos are important. If you don't do your job, you will get fired. If you don't pay your car payment, the bank will take the car away from you. If you don't balance your checkbook and review bank statements, you may bounce a check. If you aren't nice to those around you, you will pay the price.

INTERNET

www.daytimer.com

Visit this web site to find out more about the full range of Day-Timer products and to obtain contact information and order forms.

But where is the time for you to get the "want-to" items done – those things you really want to accomplish in any of your seven vital areas that I told you about in Chapter 2? Is there a book you've been itching to read or a pottery class you want to take? Have you always wanted to take up rock climbing? Do you want to finally get your investment portfolio organized? Have you resolved to make Wednesday nights family night? Make those items a part of your to-do list as well.

■ **Just think of all** *the fun things you can do if you make the time for them. Why should your interests take a back seat to your work commitments?*

Parkinson's Law

I don't know who Parkinson was but he must have been very important because he had a law named after him. It states, in part, that a project tends to expand with the time allocated for it. If you give yourself one thing to do during the day, it may take all day to complete it (depending on the task, of course). True? If you give yourself two things to do during the day, you may get both done. If you assign yourself 12 things to do during the day, you may not get all 12 done, but you may get nine done. The point is, having a lot to do tends to create a certain level of urgency so that we get more done.

There is an old expression that says, "If you want to get something done, give it to the busiest person." There's a lot of truth in that. Busy people usually know how to organize their time to get things done.

By having a lot to do, you almost automatically become more organized and a better time manager. You have to, to get it all done. People who have a lot to do in their day tend not to tolerate interruptions that may throw them off track. They tend to not waste much time in meetings. They delegate more effectively. They are more focused and attuned to leveraging their time.

■ **Delegating is a skill** *that has to be learned in order to implement it successfully. Make sure that those you are delegating to are capable of what you are asking of them, otherwise the exercise will be pointless.*

Planning your day

Here are two rules that might be helpful for you in taking advantage of Parkinson's Law:

 Overplan your days. By overplanning your days, you will take advantage of Parkinson's Law.

 Don't overplan your days.

Wait a minute! Which is it: Overplan your days or don't overplan your days? Yes, there is a conflict here and I do it only to make a point.

It's a good idea to overplan your day a bit. That means purposely scheduling more tasks and appointments than you feel comfortable managing. This creates a healthy sense of pressure to get more done in your day. But look, you're only human. Things do take time. You can only accomplish a certain amount each day and you will leave undone far more than you ever get done.

A handy tip

I recommend overplanning your day by a factor of +50 percent. Assign yourself about 50 percent more than you think you can handle during the day. This will create a healthy sense of pressure on you, but not overwhelm you at the end of the day with all the items you did not finish. For example, if you are looking at an 8-hour block of time, schedule 12 hours of things to do for that period. You probably won't get them all done, but you may get the majority done and still feel that you've accomplished a great deal. There's a lot of satisfaction in being able to cross out items on a to-do list as you get them done. Any leftover items can be forwarded to the next day's to-do list.

■ **Over-estimating what you** *can achieve in a day gives you something to strive for, but don't add too much to your to-do list, the object is to give yourself some pressure, not a heart attack.*

TO-DO LIST

Take a look at this sample to-do list for one day. Note that it includes both "have-to" and "want-to" items.

Must do	Completed
Call Allan	
Call Mom	✓
Pay bills	
Buy groceries	
Write ads for marketing program	
Balance checkbook	✓
Read a chapter	
Make dentist appointment	
Write out invitations for Susan's birthday party	
Wash car	✓
Finish work report	
Fax report to Bill	✓
Back up computer	

STEP 3: MAKE UP YOUR TO-DO LIST

Using your tool of choice, paper or electronic, take a moment now to make up your own to-do list. List all the things you have to do and all the things you want to do over the next 24 hours. You may develop a list of a dozen items or even more – in fact, the more things you can list, the better. Don't feel overwhelmed as you create your list. You will have time for the have-to items and the want-to items, as you will see in Chapter 4.

■ **A list is better** *than a confused mind – you will be so much clearer about what you want to do if you organize your thoughts on paper.*

A simple summary

✓ Don't clutter your mind with all the details of what you need to get done. Instead, take advantage of the power of the pen and write out a daily plan.

✓ A tank operator without a general will spin his wheels in activity and may sacrifice his or her productivity. Be the general and take control over your time.

✓ A to-do list is a crucial step to organizing your life as you put before you all that you have to do and all that you want to do.

✓ Overplan your day; this will give you a sense of pressure to achieve all that's on your list.

✓ Step 3 for organizing your life is to create a daily to-do list.

Chapter 4

Managing Those Competing Priorities

I WISH I COULD MAKE EVERYONE HAPPY. I feel that I disappoint some people because I never have enough time to do everything. The truth is, you will never please everyone or get everything done, but you can get the most important things done. To do this, you have to sift through what is crucial and what is not crucial. Focusing your attention on getting the most important things done will advance your successes. I really believe most people want to be good time managers. It makes sense. The more we accomplish, the more success we will enjoy, and in order to do this you need to get your prorities in order.

In this chapter...

✓ Deciding what's crucial and what's not crucial

✓ A simple prioritizing system

✓ It's a stress reducer

✓ Step 4: Prioritize your to-do list

FIGURE OUT WHAT YOU NEED TO DO FIRST – DON'T TRY TO DO IT ALL AT ONCE

Deciding what's crucial and what's not crucial

AS YOU PREPARE your to-do list each night to plan for the following day, listing not only what you have to do but also what you want to do, you'll find that some of the items on your list are more important than others. Those items that are most important – that will give you the biggest pay-off for the time invested – are crucial. Everything else you can label as not crucial.

Let's say it's the start of your day and you have before you a list of things to be done, some of which are crucial, some of which are not crucial. Intuitively and instinctively, you and I want to be good time managers, right? Therefore, where does our attention gravitate toward, the crucial or the not crucial? "The crucial," you say? Sure, it's only logical that we would select the crucial items over the not-so-crucial.

But for most of us, that does not occur. When faced with a choice between working on a crucial item or a not-crucial item, most people will select the not-crucial item. "But that defies logic," you suggest. It sure does. But you and I are driven not so much by our logic as by our emotion.

■ **Sort out all your** *jumbled thoughts last thing at night by listing and prioritizing the things that you want to do – or have to do – the next day, and look the list over first thing in the morning before you start work.*

When given a choice between doing a crucial task and a not-so-crucial task, most people will work on the not-so-crucial task first. Why? It is typically easier, quicker, and maybe a bit more fun than the crucial task.

We are guided by logic and emotion

The crucial items are typically long and may be difficult to achieve. The not-crucial items may be quicker and more fun to do. A crucial item for me might be to work on a productivity report – what is usually a long, tedious, and difficult task. Also on my desk is some junk mail to go through. It's quicker and easier for me to go through the junk mail than to work on a productivity report and so I do that first, substituting the quantity for the quality, replacing business with "busyness." (There's much more about prioritizing tasks later in this chapter.)

■ **It's much more fun** *to make a personal call than to get down to work and face that report you've been trying to forget for the last few days.*

Trivia...

Mondays are so universally dreaded we even have a name for them: "Blue Mondays." Tune in to any radio station on a Monday morning and you'll probably hear the disk jockey talking about "getting back into the rat race." One of my neighbors even sports a bumper sticker on his car that reads "I just had a whole week's worth of Mondays."

How most people plan

Many people don't do any daily planning the night before, as I outlined in Chapter 3. They may look forward to their time off more than their work time and therefore make more plans for that personal time. During our off time, we have more choices and control over our lives. Also, many people feel especially pressured at the start of the working week when they think about all they have to accomplish. By the time many of us get to work on Monday morning, we are stressed. And when we are stressed, we crave emotional relief.

■ How often have *you decided to have just one more cup of tea or coffee – the ultimate delaying tactic – before getting on with the task at hand?*

So to my left is that productivity report. And while it is crucial, it is long and difficult. To my right is that junk mail, which is not crucial, but quick and easy to take care of. So it makes sense to go the junk mail route first. Having done that, I look at that productivity report again, but I don't have coffee. I don't know about you, but I can't work without a cup of coffee. So I go to where the coffee machine is located and while getting my coffee, I have an extended chit-chat with my fellow workers about their weekend and their plans for the week ahead. Not crucial time for sure.

Okay. I have read the junk mail and I have my coffee and now I should attend to that productivity report, but I notice that my desk is a little dusty. So I get out a dust rag and some spray wax and start cleaning and polishing my desk. And so it goes. The interesting thing about this is that whichever way you start your day, whether it is in the crucial vein or a not-so-crucial vein, there's a good probability that you will slot yourself into that role for the rest of the day.

Starting your day on the right foot sets the tone for the rest of the day. Start your day with the crucial items. But if there are quick tasks you can get out of the way easily, do those first.

■ You are less *likely to have a productive day if you start it off on the wrong foot by chatting with coworkers, or reading junk e-mail rather than getting on with pressing tasks.*

Realistic aims

Let me ask you two questions. Would you like to say that at the end of each workday, you got everything done? Most would answer "yes." And can you really say that every night when you go home, you got everything done? Probably not. As I've said, we never really get it all done.

But when our goal is to get everything done, it forces us over to the not-crucial side of our to-do list, where the items are quicker and easier to accomplish. Get rid of the old rule of accomplishing everything. It's a silly rule, and you can't achieve it anyway. The new rule is "I want to get the most important things done." Ask yourself what is more valuable, getting 25 unimportant, not-crucial, items done, or 5 important crucial items? It's the 5 important crucial items.

The things you do not do in your day and your life do not count. Your productivity is never measured by what you have left undone. Your productivity is measured only by what you do get done.

■ **What better feeling** *is there than knowing you had a really productive day at work?. Learn to prioritize your tasks effectively, and you will find that you achieve so much more!*

The 20/80 rule

The **20/80 rule** (sometimes flipped and referred to as the 80/20 rule) is formally known as the Pareto Principle. It states that 80 percent of business comes from 20 percent of the customers. Vilfredo Pareto (1848–1923) was an Italian economist who discovered that about 20 percent of the companies in an economy were responsible for about 80 percent of the then Gross National Product of a country. The other 80 percent of the companies made up the other 20 percent of the Gross National Product.

> **⌐ DEFINITION ⌐**
>
> *The **20/80 rule** or Pareto Principle states that 80 percent of business comes from 20 percent of the customers. You can use the 20/80 rule to help prioritize your actions.*

Now this is not a book about macroeconomics, but the 20/80 rule has a lot of application to us as we get better at organizing our lives. Have you ever noticed that about 20 percent of a sales force produces 80 percent of the total sales? If you belong to a church or a civic association, do you find that 20 percent of the membership is there 80 percent of the time doing 80 percent of the work, while the other 80 percent of the membership shows up 20 percent of the time? Do you find that 20 percent of your relatives give you 80 percent of your headaches?

It may not always work with great mathematical precision, but typically a 20 percent effort, or the smaller chunk of your input, will produce 80 percent of your results. Later in this book, you'll find that on average, 20 percent of your time spent now is producing

80 percent of your results. If you want to double your results in life, you need not put in twice the time. All you need to do is isolate and identify how much of your time you are already spending on the things that you do so well, that produces the most payback, and then find more time to do more of what you do so well. I will share with you all the tools you will need to accomplish this.

■ **Although you may want** *your home to look perfect 100 percent of the time, you know it's impossible, so you accept a lesser standard of perfection. Apply the same principle to your work: Although you may strive for 100 percent perfection, learn to be happy with 80.*

The curse of perfectionism

Perfectionism – that pressure you may put on yourself to do everything perfectly – may be keeping you from organizing your life. Here's how it works. Most of us approach any task – cleaning the basement, preparing a term paper, writing a project for work – with the idea that we will put in 20 percent of our time to achieve 80 percent of the result. We are satisfied with that and move on. For example, let's say you spend 2 hours preparing a report for school or work. That 2 hours represents 20 percent of the potential effort; that is, by spending 2 hours on the report you are accomplishing 80 percent of the result. Sure, it could get better, it may not be perfect, but it accomplishes what needs to be done. Most of us approach tasks in this way, putting in a reasonable amount of time for a reasonable effort.

Those who suffer from the curse of perfectionism say to themselves, "Well, 80 percent of the potential result is not enough. I have to achieve a 100 percent result. This has to be perfect." This sets an unrealistic goal in and of itself, because there is probably no such thing as true perfection. No matter how many times you rewrite your report, as good as it has become, it can always get better.

So here's the problem. We have put in 2 hours to achieve 80 percent of the potential result. Now to get the additional 20 percent of potential results, we have to put in an additional 80 percent of time, or another 8 hours. That means that this additional 20 percent of results is 32 times more expensive than the initial effort. The greater problem that is the more we spend on any one thing, the less time we have for everything else.

■ **Don't set unrealistic,** *unattainable goals for yourself. Recognize what is possible to achieve in the time you have available – you will only end up feeling like a failure if you put too much pressure on yourself.*

To help avoid the trap of the curse of perfectionism, it's important to set time limits. For example, if you are going to clean up a basement, let's say you set 2 hours as the limit. Will the basement be cleaned in 2 hours? Yes. Will it be perfect? No. Can you put in more time? Sure. Can you spend all day on this one task? Yes. But then nothing else will get done.

If you set a reasonable standard in advance, once you achieve it, you can move on to something else. Without a preset standard, more never seems to be enough.

■ **There are a lot** *of things that you want to do in a day, so limit the amount of time you spend on each one – and stop fighting the clock.*

A simple prioritizing system

IF I TAKE THE TOP SHEET OFF *a pad of paper and take it outdoors and leave it there, after a while, maybe several days, the sheet will get yellow, dirty, and eventually be destroyed. Or I can take a full pad of paper with 50 sheets, go outdoors and with a magnifying glass, get a concentration of the sun's rays and destroy the entire pad in one day. In fact, I can destroy several pads of paper in one day with my magnifying glass.*

Whether I try to burn up a pad one sheet at a time or burn up a complete pad with the use of my magnifying glass, the sun does not care. It's just there for all of us and we chose how to use it. The most successful people have a device, like a magnifying glass, to help get a concentration of their resources available to magnify their results.

■ **Try to figure out** *what you can use to bring the things you need to do into focus.*

Ordering your tasks

The following *prioritizing system* can act as a sort of magnifying glass for you, a kind of filtering process that allows you to prioritize your tasks. Assign each item on your to-do list one of the following letters:

DEFINITION

*A **prioritizing system** is any tool that helps to identify your tasks in order of their importance, permitting you to focus your attention on the most important items first, saving the less important items for later.*

A **Crucial.** You are the only one who can determine which items on your list are A items. You do that by considering your commitments and responsibilities to other people, as well as in light of the balance you are trying to achieve and your personal goals.

B **Important.** While these items are important, they're not as crucial as A items. If you had a choice between an A and a B task, you would want to work on the A task.

C **Little value.** If you have an extensive to-do list you may not get to your C items today, but that's okay. Remember, your productivity is not measured by what is left over at the end of the day, but by what you actually did accomplish in your day.

D **No value.** What do you do if you find you have a D on your list? Get rid of it, because by definition it has no value. For example, you may have as a task on your to-do list to read some technical journals that have been laying around your desk, only to find out they are outdated and therefore of no value to you. If you have never written down everything you have to do and want to do, you may find you have a lot of D items on your list. What a great feeling to cross them off and get them off your back!

* **Quick.** Some items on your list may take very little time to complete. Perhaps it's a phone call or some papers you need to file. In the time it would take to figure out its value, you could have completed the task. Assign these quick and easy tasks an asterisk (*).

■ **Getting a simple task,** *such as a routine phone call, out of the way first, enables you to focus on the more important jobs of your day.*

It's a stress reducer

YOU'VE PROBABLY *heard people say that there is good stress and bad stress. In Chapter 3 I told you how deliberately putting more tasks on your to-do list will actually help make you more productive. That's a kind of good stress. But too much stress can be a killer, limiting your daily productivity and shortening your life.*

■ **If stress is affecting** *your performance at work, perhaps it's time to stop putting so much pressure on yourself.*

Most stress is caused by differences between our expectations on one level and the reality on a lower level. When we have a reality that falls short of our expectations, we feel disappointment, and that disappointment breeds stress.

Here's a simple example. Let's assume you drove your car to work this morning and parked in the employee parking lot. At the end of the workday you expect that your car will be where you left it. What if you return to the parking lot to the reality that your car is gone? Do you suppose you may experience some stress over your stolen car? On the other hand, if you return to the parking lot after work and find your car is exactly where you parked it that morning, do you experience any stress? Of course not. Why? Because your expectation and the reality matched up.

Reducing stress

How then do you reduce your stress? You have two options. Either reduce your expectations or increase your reality. My preference is to increase the reality. One way to do that is to plan your days. List all the things you have to do and all the things you want to do. Overload your day, taking advantage of Parkinson's Law (see Chapter 3). Prioritize that list and rank each item with an A, B, C, D, or * using the prioritizing system that I told you about earlier in this chapter. Then each day, complete those items on your list in the order that will give you the biggest pay-off for the time invested.

■ **Don't be afraid** *to turn to your boss if you feel stressed at work – your well-being is in his or her best interest.*

If you feel so much stress that you're having trouble sleeping at night or it's starting to affect your relationship with your family or your coworkers, it's time to do something about it. You might talk with your boss about delegating some of your responsibilities, for example.

The first step is to identify the quickie items, the items marked with an * that can be done in less than a minute or two. Next, identify the A items (crucial), B items (important), and C items (little value). Anything left over is a D item (no value); cross those off your list.

■ **Start prioritizing** *your to-do list and see how easy it is to get more done.*

Sub-prioritize

Now go back to the A items and sub-prioritize them. If you could work on only one A item, which would it be? Label that item as A-1. Then, if you have time, what is the next item you would work on? That becomes A-2. Continue through your A items, then repeat the process for your B and C items.

The following sample to-do list from Chapter 3 shows a priority assigned to each task.

TO-DO LIST

Priority	Must do	Completed
B-1	Call Allan	
B-2	Call Mom	
B-3	Pay bills	
B-4	Buy groceries	
A-1	Write ads for marketing program	
B-5	Balance checkbook	
A-2	Read one chapter	
*	Make dentist appointment	✓
C-1	Write out invitations for Susan's birthday party	
C-2	Wash car	
A-3	Finish work report	
*	Fax report to Bill	✓
*	Back up computer	✓

At the start of your day, do the * items (quick tasks) first. As you complete each task, cross it off your list. It's interesting, but that simple act of crossing off an item provides you with a level of satisfaction that keeps you motivated to go on to the next task. Then direct your attention to your A-1. Complete it and cross it off. Move on to your A-2, continuing down your list doing the tasks in order of their importance.

At the end of your day, move all the unfinished items over to the next appropriate day when you think you will be able to get them done, so that they don't get lost through the cracks.

STEP 4:
PRIORITIZE YOUR TO-DO LIST

In Chapter 3 you created your to-do list, a compilation of all the things you have to do and all the things you want to do. Now apply the prioritizing system so you can focus in on the items that will yield the best use of your time.

■ **Everyone's priorities** *are different – family, work, social life – make sure you know where yours lie.*

A simple summary

✔ When determining what tasks are crucial and not crucial, consider your commitments and responsibilities to others, as well as the balance and personal goals you are trying to achieve.

✔ A simple prioritizing system is to assign each task an A (crucial), B (important), C (little value), D (no value), or * (quick).

✔ Prioritizing tasks is actually a stress reducer because you bring reality more in line with your expectations.

✔ Remember to pencil in any unfinished tasks to the next day's to-do list.

✔ Step 4 for organizing your life is to prioritize the tasks on your to-do list.

Chapter 5

Organizing Scheduled Events

IN ADDITION TO making up your daily to-do list and prioritizing your tasks, you need to keep track of appointments and scheduled events. These include staff meetings, meetings with your boss or vendors, or perhaps a telephone appointment with an important customer. They also include personal commitments such as a dinner engagement, dentist appointment, evening class, concert, or hair appointment. In this chapter I'll show you a simple system for keeping track of all of your personal and professional commitments.

In this chapter...

✔ *The holistic approach: use one calendar*

✔ *Get a full month at a glance*

✔ *Step 5: Create your calendar of scheduled events*

KEEP TRACK OF ALL YOUR APPOINTMENTS SO YOU DON'T MISS AN IMPORTANT APPOINTMENT

The holistic approach: use one calendar

THERE ARE SEVERAL DIFFERENT ways to manage
appointments and scheduled events. Some people write them down
on a wall calendar or desk blotter; others carry a pocket calendar;
others just try to keep track of their appointments in their
heads. Many people keep separate calendars for work
appointments and personal commitments. The problem is,
one area of our life affects the other. We need a holistic
approach. I recommend carrying one calendar with you
and using it for everything, both business and personal
appointments. This simple approach gives you the most
control and is the easiest to use.

INTERNET

www.scheduleonline.
com

*ScheduleOnline is an online
calendar that enables you to
keep track of your work and
social schedules 24 hours a
day, 7 days a week. Useful
features include a To-Do list,
and you can share
information with family,
friends, and colleagues.*

Choose a calendar that's small enough to
carry around with you in your purse or briefcase.
That way you can always refer to it when
booking appointments.

Get a full month at a glance

THE BEST TYPE OF CALENDAR I have used is one that gives me a
full month at a glance, such as the sample calendar shown opposite. This
permits me to see the big picture, not just one day at a time. By using a
full-month-at-a-glance system, I receive three important benefits: I get to
take advantage of context, anticipation, and integration. Let's take a closer
look at each of these benefits.

JUNE 2001

Sunday	Monday	Tuesday	Wednesday	Thursday	Friday	Saturday
					1 9 a.m. Bob – meeting	2 4 – 7 p.m. BBQ
3	4 10 a.m. client meeting	5 6 p.m. Simon	6	7 11 a.m. photocopier service	8 12.30 p.m. Harry – lunch	9 8.30 a.m. children swimming
10	11	12 10.30 a.m. budget papers 6 p.m. movies	13 9 a.m. symposium	14	15	16
17	18	19	20	21 12 p.m. interview	22 pick up dry cleaning 7 p.m. dinner – Jo	23 2 p.m. bank

■ **By inserting all** *scheduled events, both work and social, into your calendar, you will be able to see exactly what you should be doing when, and avoid double-booking yourself.*

Context

You want to schedule your appointments in the context of what is going on around them. For example, let's say you get a call from a client who wants to meet with you on Friday the 10th at 2 p.m. to discuss time-management issues. If you look at your schedule for that day only, perhaps the time slot is available, so you would be inclined to agree to the request for a meeting.

Most of us schedule our commitments based on our availability. When someone is asking of our time, if we are available we are inclined to say yes. Why? Because we have been trained to say yes to please and to accommodate. We don't get too far in this world by saying no all the time.

■ **Use your time wisely** – *if you can rearrange a meeting so it suits you better, then why not do so?*

Don't overcommit

Now there's nothing wrong with making that commitment for Friday the 10th at 2 p.m., but maybe there is a better way. Refer to your calendar for the full month so you can see what is going on not only on the 10th, but the day before, the day after, the week before, and the week after. As you schedule appointments, take into account what may already be scheduled before and after this new event and allow yourself enough time to get from one commitment to the next.

Is there an alternative?

Let's say that on Saturday the 11th, you and your family are leaving on a one-week skiing vacation. If you're like most people, your mind is not 100 percent focused on business the day before you leave for a vacation. Of course, you want to be able to give your client 100 percent of your attention, so it does not make good sense to schedule that important meeting for Friday the 10th. You might suggest meeting instead on Wednesday the 8th. Chances are the earlier date will work just as well for your client.

■ **Check your schedule** *to make sure that you don't over-commit to too many meetings in too little time.*

When someone asks for your time, there is usually an alternative date and time that will work just as well. Of course it depends on the nature of the meeting, but most of the time this is true.

When your client asked for Friday the 10th and you are able to move the appointment to Wednesday the 8th, who is in control? You are. And I don't mean you are in control in any evil or manipulative way. Your client gets the appointment with you that she wants, and you schedule it at a time that makes more sense in the context of what else is going on in your week.

■ **Be realistic** – *if you know your concentration isn't going to be 100 percent during an important meeting, because of personal reasons, reschedule the meeting.*

Rationalize your schedule

Let's look at another example. Let's say Friday the 10th is clear and you have no vacation plans. Your client's office is located about a half-hour from yours. To get there and back is an hour's commuting time. As you look at your full-month-at-a-glance calendar, you notice that you have another appointment already set up with another client in the same area one week later on Friday the 17th. It sure makes good sense to combine both appointments and kill two birds with one stone. Suggest to your client: "Yes, I could meet with you on Friday the 10th, but I'm already scheduled to be in your area the following Friday on the 17th. How about if we meet on the afternoon of the 17th?" If the client is available at that time, there's a good chance he will agree.

Two trips for the price of one

Let's say you suggest an alternative date and time and the client firmly replies, "No. You either be here on Friday the 10th or no deal!" Well, you're a reasonable person. And so you will make two trips to the same place on consecutive Fridays. That's what you were going to do anyway, so you're no worse off. But here's an idea. If your client can't move the appointment from Friday the 10th to Friday the 17th, how about calling the other client to see if the appointment on the 17th could be moved up one week?

■ **Don't face two journeys** *when you can make one – think about your schedule carefully and make time work for you.*

A question of personality

Context also deals with personality styles. For example, there are morning people and there are night people. Morning people are at their most productive during the morning hours. Night people function more productively later in the day. (Then there are those who are no darn good any time of the day!)

It is easier to flow downstream with the current than to try to buck the flow of the water. Go with your natural strengths and rhythms.

■ **If you're not a "morning person,"** *try to schedule your meetings and appointments for the afternoon.*

I am more of a night person. My energy level goes up later in the day than early in the morning. Knowing this, I try to schedule important events and meetings for later in the day. On the other hand, if I were a morning person, I would want to schedule important meetings for early in the day.

Another personal style is a racehorse and a tortoise. A racehorse thrives on overload. They like lots and lots of things going on at the same time. This is what gets their juices flowing. (If you are a racehorse, you probably crammed for your exams in school!) A tortoise is someone who likes to take on things at a more even pace, spreading them out and not getting overloaded. Racehorses and tortoises can accomplish just as much. They just do it differently.

■ **Schedule your meetings** *for a time when you know you'll be at your most productive – you know it makes sense.*

If you know that you tend to be a racehorse and you have five appointments to set up for the coming week, you may try to set up three for Monday and the other two for Tuesday. On the other hand, if you are more of a tortoise, you may wish to set up only one appointment per day and stretch them out so you don't feel overloaded.

Anticipation

Anticipation is the idea that I have one place I can see at a glance everything that is coming up tomorrow, the day after, next week, and next month so that I can plan to do things that will make future appointments and scheduled events run more smoothly.

There was a time when I did not use the full-month-at-a-glance concept. Instead, I used a day calendar and managed scheduled events for that day only. The rest were buried in the other pages of my daily calendar so I was dealing with just today's appointments and not considering what was coming up tomorrow and the next day.

Learning the hard way

One Friday afternoon around 2 p.m., Lori, my assistant at the time, came into my office and said, "Well, I guess we won't be seeing you for the next couple of weeks." That was right. The following day I was leaving on a 2-week family camping trip. Now I knew I was going away, but it wasn't uppermost in my mind. What I was focusing on was that day's problems, not thinking ahead. So all the things I needed to get done before I could leave – items that could have been done earlier in the week – had to be dealt with then. I kept Lori there that Friday night until around 7 p.m., assigning things to her that I easily could have done earlier in the week if I had been thinking ahead.

■ **Let your coworkers** *know in advance if you are going to be away – they can plan for your absence and reassign anything that needs to be done urgently.*

Don't forget to plan ahead. If you fail to manage your time, you not only limit your own productivity and success, you negatively impact on others as well.

Lori was real happy to see me go away for 2 weeks at this point. She probably thought, "Why doesn't he go away for 3 or 4 weeks!" When people don't manage their time well they tend to have an impact on other people as well. Lori had every right to be upset with me. But I was not done at 7 p.m. – I still had bills to pay and paperwork to complete. I did not get out of my office until 11 p.m. that night. And at that time, I learned a very important lesson and it took me an hour. The lesson was, you could not buy film in the city of Shelton, Connecticut, at 11 p.m. at night. You see, as I was leaving my office, it suddenly hit me that I would need film for my vacation.

■ **Don't give yourself a headache** *by leaving everything to the last minute; anticipate what needs to be done and make sure you leave yourself plenty of time to do it.*

I got home at midnight, exhausted. Now we were supposed to be packed and ready to go at 6 a.m. to avoid all the traffic around New York City, but we are not packed. So the next morning, I'm up at 6:30 a.m., rushing to pack and feeling stressed. At 8:30 a.m., as we are going down the driveway, my wife asked, "You did get the traveler's checks, didn't you?" Whoops! Forgot about that too. Now we have to wait another half-hour for the bank to open to get the traveler's checks. We ran into all the traffic going through New York City that I had hoped to avoid. When I planned this vacation, I imagined that by around 9:30 a.m. we would all be sailing down the New Jersey Turnpike, past New York City, singing "Zippity Doo Dah," like the Griswolds in the movie National Lampoon's Vacation. But by then my wife and I were so stressed we were not even speaking to each other!

Plan ahead

Years ago, when I started law practice as a new lawyer, my boss told me three things about vacation time. First, it would always be a crunch to get out the door to start a vacation. Second, I should plan on at least 3 days to unwind. Third, when I returned after being away for a week or two, "it" would hit the fan; I would be in chaos dealing with the stuff that accumulated in my absence! And that is the way it always played out whenever we went away: a real crunch and stressful time to get away, 3 days to unwind (giving up a big piece of my vacation time to undo what I had done to myself before I left), and always, "it" would hit the fan when I returned. I always blamed my profession for this. I figured that was the price I had to pay because I chose to be an attorney, because so many of my attorney friends experienced the same difficulties. One day I realized this had little to do with being an attorney and more to do with organizing my life and being a good time manager.

■ **Simple organization** *is all that's needed to make your day run smoothly.*

Anticipation as prevention

Now all that hassle does not happen when I go away on vacation because I use the principle of anticipation to prevent it. Each night in my daily planning, I look ahead to not only what is scheduled for tomorrow, but also for the following day, the following week, and the following month. I have all my future appointments and scheduled events, both business and personal, in one location. As I look at every appointment and scheduled event coming up, I ask, "What can I do in anticipation of this event tomorrow, next week, or next month?" If I am going to a staff meeting next Thursday at 10 a.m., perhaps I can prepare an agenda to make that meeting run more smoothly. If I have a doctor's appointment for my annual physical scheduled for the last day of this month, perhaps I could make up a list of health questions that have been on my mind since we last met. If I know I'm going on vacation next week, I can do things like pack, buy film for my camera, and go to the bank for traveler's checks ahead of time.

I'm not creating any more work for myself because all of these things have to be done either sooner or later. By using the principle of anticipation, I do them sooner, at my own pace. When I wait until the deadline is upon me, I become a slave to the clock. The deadline now controls me. The stress level is up and I am rushing around, cutting corners.

A few minutes spent planning a task will pay you back 10 minutes in time saved during the actual doing of the task.

Integration

The final benefit of using a full-month-at-a-glance system is *integration*. A student in one of my time-management seminars approached me during a break after I discussed this principle of integration. He told me he had just lost a $10,000-per-year contract because of it. He was employed at a local corporation as a computer analyst and made a good salary. He also did computer-consulting work for his own clients on the side. He was also the soccer coach for a kids' soccer team. Like so many of us he had a lot of balls in the air, and he had a separate calendar to keep track of each of his commitments.

One day recently, a client of his called and asked if he would be available to do some consulting work for them in the evening on Thursday, the 20th of the month. My student went into his den where he kept his consulting calendar. The date and time were both available, so he said yes. He forgot to go into the kitchen and look on his refrigerator, where he had the kids' soccer calendar posted. The 20th happened to be the day of the championship game and he had to be there. He could not let the kids down.

> **DEFINITION**
>
> **Integration** *is the concept of having everything you need – both work and personal appointments – in one location.*

He also neglected to look at his work schedule. "Where was that?" I asked. "At work," he replied. "Why would I carry my work calendar with me in my personal life? What relevance does my work calendar have to my personal life?" Well, as it turns out, the 20th was the day that the executive vice-president of his company was flying in for a full day of special meetings. He could see that it was going to be an unusually stressful day at work.

■ **Having one calendar** *rather than two, or three, will help you to balance your work and personal commitments.*

■ **Your days of rushing to meet your appointments** *could be over if you learn to schedule your commitments wisely.*

It turned out that my student went to work on the 20th and sure enough, he had one of the most stressful days ever. He came home around 5 p.m., tired out. But he had to suit up and go across town to coach that soccer game for the kids. After the game, he rushed home, took a shower and changed clothes, and rushed again across town to get to the consulting assignment with his private client, showing up 15 minutes late and obviously exhausted.

Just a week before our seminar, my student told me he received a letter from his private client informing him that they were terminating his services. When they pay you $50 an hour, they expect their money's worth out of you. My student remarked, "It was so true. If I only practiced the principle of integration, had everything, business and personal, all in one location, there would have been no way I would have said yes to their date and time. If I had said no to the 20th and rescheduled the assignment to the following week, the client would have been agreeable. But when I said yes to their date and time, I had to perform. I could not believe how simple but powerful that technique of integration was all about."

Being organized does not mean you must reduce the number of appointments and scheduled events you have. It just means you need to maintain control over those appointments and events.

STEP 5:
CREATE YOUR CALENDAR OF SCHEDULED EVENTS

Choose a full-month-at-a-glance calendar that's small enough to carry around with you. Starting with the current month, record all of your appointments and scheduled events. Write down every business and personal time-specific commitment, including business meetings, lunches with clients, doctor's appointments, dinners, parties, and the like. Whenever you schedule an appointment or event, get in the habit of writing it down on your calendar immediately, so that you don't forget it. Keep the calendar with you at all times and refer to it often.

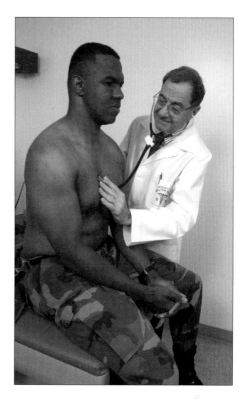

■ **Make sure you** *don't forget important events, such as a doctor's appointment, by getting in the habit of noting the date and time into your calendar as soon as you schedule an arrangement.*

A simple summary

✔ The holistic approach – using one calendar to record both personal and professional commitments – is a simple, effective way to keep track of appointments and scheduled events.

✔ Use a full-month-at-a-glance calendar so that you can take advantage of context, anticipation, and integration.

✔ Step 5 for organizing your life is to create your calendar of scheduled events.

PART TWO

Chapter 6
Crisis Management

Chapter 7
Other Useful Tools for Getting Organized

Chapter 8
Overcoming Procrastination

Chapter 9
The Importance of Delegation

Chapter 10
Specific Ways to Delegate

HURDLES ARE EASY TO OVERCOME IF YOU KNOW HOW

OVERCOMING BARRIERS AND BUILDING BLOCKS

You've learned about the big picture of time management and the importance of daily planning to take control of your to-do items and appointments and scheduled events. For some, there may be some *barriers* to overcome to take full advantage of what you have learned so far. For everyone, there are tools you can use as building blocks to *enhance* your success.

In Part Two I'll help you conquer the important barriers of crisis management and procrastination as well as give you a *boost* with some simple but powerful building blocks.

Chapter 6

Crisis Management

CRISIS MANAGEMENT HAPPENS TO EVERYONE. Have you ever discovered a deadline that has crept up on you, or left all the details of a family visit to the last minute? This is when you find yourself in crisis management mode – when you have run out of time and the clock controls you instead of the other way around. It's not a very good feeling, is it? Some crises cannot be avoided, but others, the unproductive ones, cause the most concern. We need to get these crises under our control. I'll show you how to do that in this chapter.

In this chapter...

✔ What is crisis management?

✔ Why it happens

✔ A tool to fix it: the crisis management log

✔ Most crises can be prevented

✔ Step 6: Run your crisis management log

SOME CRISES ARE UNAVOIDABLE, BUT MANY OF THEM CAN EASILY BE PREVENTED WITH A LITTLE MANAGEMENT

What is crisis management?

When you practice poor time management **crisis management** usually occurs. It's when you leave things to the last minute that are really within your control to do. Then you rush around, under pressure to get them done. When you are under pressure, your stress level goes up. You may find yourself cutting corners to get the task done. Other details may slip through the cracks. You may have to go back and redo what was done improperly in the first place because you were in such a rush to get it done.

DEFINITION

Crisis management is what results when a deadline has snuck up on you and robbed you of all choice. You are now a slave to the clock instead of being in control of your time.

Excuses, excuses

Over the years, I have been amazed at my college students who hand in term papers at the last moment and plead, "This is the best I could do. I didn't have time to do it the right way." My response has always been, "So when will you have time to redo it in the future?" It's kind of crazy, isn't it? You don't have time to do it the right way in the first place, so when are you going to get the time in the future to do it the right way?

■ **How often have** *you found yourself working late to meet that deadline?*

■ **Don't struggle in silence,** *be proactive about your workload. If it is really too much for you, there is always a solution.*

Take a look at the following two scenarios:

John did not get his raise, but it's not his fault because . . .

. . . he did not get all his work done on time because they gave him too much to do and because he was late yesterday because he had to stop for gas because he didn't stop for gas the night before because he was late coming home . . . because he was working late because he came in late that morning because he had to iron a shirt because he had nothing clean to wear because he forgot to pick up his shirts from the cleaners on his way home the day before . . .

You get the point. Even though John has the tools and techniques to better control and manage his time and life, they are uncomfortable for him to use because it is so much easier to spend the day responding to problems rather than taking the initiative to prevent them.

INTERNET

www.crisisexperts.com

If you really want to get into the heart and soul of crisis management and explore some unique approaches, visit the Institute for Crisis Management's web site.

Sue, on the other hand, did get her raise because . . .

. . . she got all of her work done on time because they gave her lots to do to help her to show off her "stuff" because she was not late yesterday because she stopped earlier for gas because she was not late coming home . . . because she was working late but got home early because she came in early that morning because she ironed her blouse the night before even though she had plenty of other clothes to wear because she remembered to pick up her clothes from the cleaners on her way home the day before . . .

Sue knows she has to manage her life first because other people's opinions of what she should be doing are not nearly as important or as accurate as her own. Sue has the tools and techniques to better control and manage her time and life, and while they are sometimes uncomfortable to use, they help her to do more of what is important in her life.

So who do you wish to be? John or Sue?

■ **Every job or profession** *has its associated pressures, and it's vital you understand those pressures, whatever they may be, in order to carry out your job as effectively as possible.*

Why it happens

CRISIS MANAGEMENT TYPICALLY *has little to do with your job, your company, or your responsibilities. Many people believe they are in the crisis mode a lot because of the nature of the work they do, but I don't believe it. After all, if a particular job or profession was prone to automatic crisis management, everyone in that job or profession throughout the world would be in crisis. As you look at any job or profession you will find some and maybe many who are in crisis management. But there are always others who are not.*

Day-to-day interruptions

One of my clients is a restaurant franchise company. One of the responsibilities of each of their franchises is to submit their sales data for the previous week to central headquarters every Wednesday by 11 a.m. The franchiser needs this data by then so that it can pump it all into its computers and do an analysis of what is selling and how effective its advertising programs are. Compliance is not optional, because if the franchiser allowed franchises to submit this information "as soon as possible" or whenever each franchise got around to it, the franchiser would never have the appropriate data to compete effectively in the marketplace.

Most of the crises we experience are caused by things that are within our control. Many can be avoided by doing a good job of daily planning each night, looking ahead at what is coming up and asking yourself what you can do in anticipation of those events.

So every Wednesday by 11 a.m., this data must be received. This requirement is so stringent that if a franchise repeatedly fails to deliver their data on time they may lose their franchise. As a result, Wednesday is a stressful day in this business for most of the franchises. About 75 percent of the franchises dread Wednesdays because they are under the gun to get their reports out by 11 a.m. Here is what typically occurs. It is Wednesday morning and the franchise owner arrives at his restaurant planning to work on that report first thing. He no sooner gets started when he gets a call from the restaurant manager that she is ill and will not be able to come to work today. Now the owner is spending time on the phone to find a replacement. Next, an employee comes into the owner's office with news that he ran out of key supplies that will be needed to serve today's customers. The owner, now in a panic, is again on the phone, talking to suppliers to get the supplies he needs, feeling the pressure of the impending deadline. Somehow, amid all the distractions, the owner manages to get the report together and off to headquarters, just under the 11 a.m. wire. What a relief – well, until next Wednesday, when the owner will repeat the same crisis.

■ **To avoid lurching** *from one crisis to another, try to anticipate potentially tricky situations and plan for them.*

■ **The best-laid plans** *require some thought. It's better to spend a half hour planning in advance than trying to deal with a chaotic situation on the spot.*

Plan for success!

Many in the restaurant franchise business would tell you that they experience this crisis management because of the nature of the business and the requirements they have to honor. Probably 75 percent of restaurant franchise owners would tell you that. But if that were true – that it's the nature of the business that creates the crisis – it would seem to follow that 100 percent of the owners would have the same experience. Sure, maybe 75 percent of them do. But 25 percent do not.

To those 25 percent, Wednesday is just like any other day. They have to submit the same reports under the same deadlines as everyone else. What is different for those 25 percent is that they use their time differently. On Monday, they make sure that they have lined up management coverage for the week and back-up coverage if the primary manager is unavailable. On Tuesday, they check to make sure they have adequate supplies on hand for their customers for the week. In other words, they plan ahead.

Each night in my daily planning, I look ahead at all the appointments and scheduled events I have committed to and all of the discretionary items I have listed on my daily to-do lists for the next several days. As I review each item, I ask myself, "What can I do today in anticipation of this appointment or to-do list item coming up tomorrow, the next day, or next week? What can I do to make it run more smoothly?" Most of the time I can always find a few things I can do to make sure future events run smoothly, and I make those improvements action items in my to-do list.

A tool to fix it: the crisis management log

SOMEONE VERY SMART once said, "A problem well defined is 95 percent solved." That makes sense, doesn't it? If you have a clear, complete picture of the nature of a problem, finding the solution is often the easy part. We need a simple tool to help us define our crisis management problem, and I have that for you in the form of a crisis management log.

Life is not perfect. Everything we discuss in this book will not work 100 percent of the time. None of us will ever establish a totally crisis-free life (and wouldn't that be boring anyway?). Despite our best efforts, the unexpected will always crop up. Our goal here is not perfection, but if you can dramatically reduce the number of crises you face, you will enhance your productivity.

Don't continue to experience the same crises over and over. Take the time to step back now and again and see which ones you can prevent.

■ **If you have experienced** *the same crisis before, try to learn from it. Look at what you did or did not do the last time, and try something new to alleviate the problem.*

Get started

There is nothing complex about the crisis management log. Just get a pad of paper and write across the top, "Crisis Management Log." Then create two columns below. To the left, create a column for "Date" and to the right, create a column for "Remarks."

As you encounter each crisis throughout your day, deal with it first and then log it into your crisis management log. Don't wait until the end of the day to record any crises that occur; if you wait that long, you're more likely to forget the details. Write down the date it occurred under the "Date" column. Record a few remarks in the "Remarks" column about what the crisis was so that several days later, when you go back and review your log, you will remember each crisis.

It's a good idea to run your crisis management log for at least 2 weeks to log in a fair sampling of your experience. If you do it for a shorter period of time, you might get a distorted view of what is really occurring.

■ **It may be time-consuming** *to track your daily crises, but doing so will yield valuable information on how you can prevent or, at the very least, reduce the number of crises in your day.*

CRISIS MANAGEMENT LOG

Take a look at this sample crisis management log.

Date	Remarks
June 1	Client call – contract did not arrive
June 1	Boss needs report this afternoon
June 2	Go to bank – forgot to make deposit to cover mortgage payment
June 3	No lunch hour – need to pick up birthday gift for Susan
June 3	Late for dinner party – getting gas in car
June 5	Late for work meeting – ironing clothes to wear
June 6	Client call – page 3 of contract missing
June 6	Office supply store late with proposal handouts
June 9	Toner cartridges for copier on backorder
June 9	Deadline moved up for Jones project
June 11	Overnight package to client did not arrive

■ **Have you ever** *noticed how missing one meeting creates a domino effect that throws off your schedule for the entire day?*

Most crises can be prevented

HAVING ACCUMULATED THE ENTRIES in your crisis management log for at least 2 weeks, you now have a lot of valuable information. You know how many crises you have experienced during a certain period. You can see if there any are repetitive crises. Many of the crises will be events beyond your control. Emergencies do happen and a lot of what you are responsible for is to handle these events as they arise. These are not your concern. You need to bring under control the repetitive crises that you can control.

Avoiding the same old problems

Do you find the same problems keep popping up over and over? For example, if you are constantly late for work because you've delayed ironing your work clothes or putting gas in the car, factor in more time to do these tasks in the morning, or better yet, do them the night before. If there is a monthly report due on the 20th of each month and you find yourself working late on the 19th of each month to get it done, schedule the time to do it several days ahead of time. These kinds of crises are easily prevented.

The most important thing you can do with the information on your log is to look at each and every crisis you found yourself facing during this period and ask yourself, "How could this crisis have been avoided?" Then commit to action. Take steps to avoid these crises from reoccurring in the future.

■ **Try and identify what** *triggers a crisis. For instance, if you are always late for work because you don't take the time to iron your clothes the night before, change your routine – and get to work on time.*

Most people discover that over half of the crises they deal with (time ran out, a deadline was upon them, or their back was against the wall) are actually events that they are capable of controlling.

STEP 6:
RUN YOUR CRISIS MANAGEMENT LOG

Schedule a time to run your crisis management log for a 2-week period. Study the results to see if you can detect any patterns, and then take corrective action to prevent those crises from reoccurring.

■ **You can prevent** *stressful situations from ocurring if you take a little time to stop and look at what causes the crises in your life.*

A simple summary

✔ Crisis management is the result of poor time management.

✔ Crisis management is partly beyond our control as there are many unexpected emergencies that come our way, but often it is the result of inadequate (or no) planning.

✔ Keeping a crisis management log gives you a specific picture of the crises you deal with daily.

✔ If you can reduce some of the repetitive crises in your life you will reduce your stress and be more productive.

✔ The solutions to crises are not usually too hard to find once you have identified the cause.

✔ Step 6 for organizing your life is to start running your crisis management log.

Chapter 7

Other Useful Tools for Getting Organized

Neat little tools, gadgets, and accessories are always helpful and so I would be remiss if I didn't include some here for you to help better organize your life. These tools don't cost much and take little effort to use, but they yield big dividends in helping to make your life more organized and productive.

In this chapter...

✓ Using index cards

✓ Keep an irritations list

✓ Make a gift list

✓ Address and phone directory

✓ Improving the job each day

✓ A portable file cabinet

✓ Step 7: Start using these useful tools

Using index cards

THERE ARE A LOT OF LITTLE things in life that we can easily overlook. One simple solution for keeping track of all the details is to carry around a bunch of 3 x 5 index cards. You can pick these up at your local office supply or department store. Label and use the cards to remind yourself of all those small things that might ordinarily slip through the cracks. This is one way of keeping yourself organized that is inexpensive and takes very little effort.

For example, I have a 3 x 5 card labeled "Books to pick up." When I hear about an interesting book I might want to get, I add it to that card. I don't just drop everything and rush to the bookstore. I file the card away in my Day-Timer. The next time I'm at the mall, perhaps waiting for my wife to finish her shopping, I look in my Day-Timer, which I always keep with me, and check my booklist card. Then I go into the bookstore and get the one or two titles from my list.

Write it down!

One of my hobbies is to collect 45 rpm records, stuff from the 1950s and 1960s. I have perhaps 300 or so records that I have picked up here and there over the years. (I'm told that the record companies no longer use the 45 rpm record format so as the years go by, perhaps my collection will develop some real value!) I might be out driving one afternoon and an old song comes on the radio. "I need to get that!" I exclaim. The problem is, if I don't have a place to write it down, I'll probably forget the title. So, I have another 3 x 5 index card labeled "Records to pick up." When I'm near a record store I can pick up a record or two to add to my collection. It's that simple.

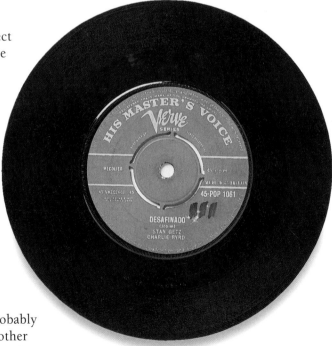

■ **Make a note** of the items you are interested in collecting, such as rare 45 rpm records – and don't miss out on a bargain again!

I have another 3 x 5 card for "Words to look up" to help me improve my vocabulary. Whenever I come across a new word, I add it to this list and when I get the opportunity, I look up the definition in the dictionary. It's kind of fun and it does improve my vocabulary a lot with a little effort.

Carry your Day-Timer (or whatever tool you use to manage your time) with you at all times so that you can take advantage of little opportunities to better organize your life.

■ **Keep a list of books** *you want to read so that the next time you visit a bookstore, you know exactly what to look for.*

Make a wish list

I have another 3 x 5 card for "Staples," my favorite office supply store. As I run out of office supplies, I add them to this list. When the list gets long enough, I make the trip to the store to pick up a lot of things at once rather than making frequent trips for a few items. It's more productive and frees up my time for more important things.

I have another 3 x 5 card with the heading "Video list." My wife and I enjoy movies a lot and I enjoy renting movies from our local video store. When I hear about a new movie being released on video, I add it to my list. Then, the next time I visit the video rental store, I can pick up one or two videos I know we will enjoy rather than spending a lot of time browsing. Without this kind of simple system, I could easily spend a half hour or more searching for a video that captures my interest. Often times I would just get impatient with this search process and select a compromise choice. Not only am I saving time, I'm seeing the movies I really want to see.

You may not be interested in books, records, movies, and the things I like to track. But whatever is slipping through the cracks in your days, use the 3 x 5 card system to capture it. By using the power of the pen and getting the small stuff down on paper, you are freeing your brain for the important things.

Keep an irritations list

WE ALL HAVE IRRITATIONS, big and small. We once owned a van that we used in my speaking business and for family use. Shortly after I got it, the gas gauge broke. It always showed the tank as empty. We eventually fixed it with a phone call to the dealer and $35, but until I got around to it, I would start this van every morning and remind myself that the gas gauge needed to be fixed. Then I would forget about it until the next morning. Every time I filled up the gas tank, I had to remember to reset the odometer because I could only get about 200 miles (320 km) to a tank of gas. But then I would wonder, did I reset it the last time I got gas? Am I going to run out of gas?

This is a good example of the unnecessary stress we sometimes build into our lives. This is the type of irritation you want to put on your irritations list, so you can begin the process of taking control of the problem, so it does not wind up controlling you.

Some annoying things in life are beyond our control and we have to adjust to them. However, there are many annoying things that, upon reflection, are within our control to change.

■ **Think of the things** *that irritate you the most – the car breaking down at inopportune moments, for example – and consider how you can stop this from happening in the future.*

Don't continue to suffer the annoying things if you can fix them. Life is too short to pay that price.

Take action against irritations

I had another little irritation. The sink in my bathroom was not draining adequately and every morning as I brushed my teeth, the water and all that was being dumped into the sink would back up. It was like brushing my teeth in a puddle outdoors. And every morning I would curse at this and proclaim that something had to be done. I endured this for several weeks until I finally remembered to pick up a can of drain cleaner at the store. What was so silly was I had been using the irritations list for some time at that point.

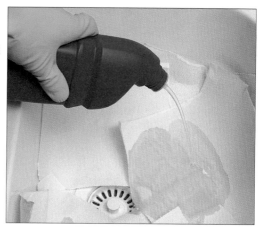

■ **Take care of minor irritations** *in your life, such as a blocked sink, instead of letting them bog you down.*

Life is not perfect, and neither am I when I fail to heed my own advice! Anyway, the point is to put these little annoyances on your irritations list. They are like pebbles in your shoe – but it's these pebbles that make the walk uncomfortable. Periodically in your daily planning, review your irritations list and commit to taking action on some or all of the items to eliminate them from your life. Whatever you choose to do to eliminate an irritation, put it in your Day-Timer as an action statement on the day when you think you'll get to it.

Make a gift list

HAVE YOU EVER OVERLOOKED *an important birthday or anniversary? We often have to pay big time for that oversight. I used to try to remember these important dates in my head but wound up forgetting them most of the time. I later used a separate calendar just for birthdays and anniversaries, which was a good idea except I would forget to look at it a lot of the time.*

■ **Transfer all your important,** *not-to-be forgotten dates onto your master calendar and you'll never forget another birthday again.*

Making sure you never forget

Then I came up with a sure-fire system for remembering these important dates. Here's how it works. Make a list of all the birthdays and anniversaries you need to track during the entire year. Put the list on a 3 x 5 index card in chronological order.

Trivia...

I was always terrible at remembering birthdays and anniversaries. I was always sending belated birthday and anniversary cards. My oversight always made me feel guilty.

Then paper-clip the list in your Day-Timer a couple of weeks before the next date you want to acknowledge. A few weeks before the next important date, open your Day-Timer, and there is the birthday and anniversary index card. For example, you see that your sister's birthday is coming up in about 2 weeks. What would you like to do in celebration of her birthday? Call her? Send a present or a card? Whatever it is you want to do, put that down as an action item on the day you think you'll get to it. Then move your 3 x 5 birthday and anniversary index card forward and paper-clip it again in your Day-Timer to about 2 weeks before that next date.

Since I've used this system, I never miss an important birthday and anniversary, whereas before I was not too good about it. And I never have to go through the exercise of writing down all the dates at the beginning of each year for that year, which not only takes time but also increases the probability of error.

Year-round planning

Some of us are born to shop, while others are not. I am one who is not. I used to dread Christmas because it meant I had to go shopping for a Christmas present for my wife. I would spend hours going up and down the aisles in the big department stores. The problem was, I would eventually run out of patience and select something that wasn't particularly special. Then on Christmas morning, my wife would open her present and say, "Oh . . . another pair of pink slippers with the bunny ears on top." She was not being ungrateful; it's just that my gift-giving was not all that creative.

■ **Finding the perfect gift** *for someone you care about is not impossible, if you plan ahead.*

It's tough to find what you want when you don't know what you're looking for. When you don't know where you're going, you don't know when you've arrived.

I have that one solved. On January 1 of each year I make up another 3 x 5 index card that says "Nancy's Christmas" and I paper-clip it to the last day of the month in the current Day-Timer I am carrying. This way it's with me all year long.

I am amazed at the ideas for gift-giving that I come across throughout the year and when I do, I put it on the list. Perhaps it's the middle of July and Nancy is looking at a mail order catalog. She observes, "Look at this sweater. Isn't it pretty? Green. I like that green." She's not fishing for a gift. She's just making an observation. When she is done with that catalog, I put the information for ordering that sweater on my Christmas list so that by December 1 of each year, I have my Christmas list all made up. Then Christmas shopping isn't such a chore. I can easily call and order some gifts and know which stores to go to for others. Being organized in this way saves time and aggravation, and the quality of my gift-giving is enhanced. Christmas morning Nancy opens her present and exclaims, "Oh, the sweater! And it's green, my favorite color! How did you know I wanted this?" "Because I'm a genius," I reply.

No, I'm not really a genius. I just have some simple tools that save me some time and help me to look better in the eyes of others. You can use them too.

■ **Even if you are not a born shopper,** *you can transform the annual Christmas shopping trip into an enjoyable day on the town; all it takes is a little planning.*

Address and phone directory

ANOTHER NEAT AND VALUABLE TOOL *is a pocket address and phone directory. You can get one at any office supply store. My address and phone directory is about 3 x 6 inches and fits nicely in my Day-Timer. I call it my flat Rolodex. What is good about these little books is that you can put in a lot of names, addresses, and phone numbers. Mine holds about 250 of the names, addresses, and phone numbers that I need on a regular basis. I do a lot of traveling, but even when I work out of my office I refer to it several times during the day.*

Many people use an electronic device such as a Palm Pilot to accomplish the same purpose. These are great because they can hold a lot more data and do a lot more than a paper address and phone directory. The only problem is, it's another thing you have to lug around.

Saving yourself hours of time

It does take a while to load up this address and phone directory with names, addresses, and phone numbers, but what a powerful tool it becomes in keeping you organized and saving you time! Without it, I was always scrambling through files and telephone directories or calling directory assistance to locate telephone numbers I needed at the moment, only to look up the same numbers a few days later. The time I spent organizing information in my phone and address book saves me even more time whenever I use it.

■ **Transfer addresses** *and phone numbers to a portable system, such as a small notebook, so that you can have them with you at all times.*

Huge increases in your overall productivity can come from small improvements. If you organize your phone and address information and it saves you only 5 minutes a day, you will save 35 minutes a week, and over 30 hours during the next year.

Travel assistance

I also have other information in my address and phone directory that I like having at my fingertips. I have all my frequent flyer numbers for all the different airlines I use. My travel agent is great but occasionally he will forget to log in my frequent flyer number for a trip when he books my reservation. Then after the trip was over, it would occur to me I did not get credit for the miles flown. This is not a showstopper. I could make a copy of boarding passes and write to the airline to get the miles credited to my account, but there's one more thing to keep track of and spend time on.

■ **If you are a frequent traveler**, *your trips will be less stressful and more pleasant if you keep important numbers on hand.*

■ **Business trips can be stressful,** *so save yourself unnecessary aggravation by taking care of the little details beforehand. Relax and enjoy the ride.*

Now when I travel, I always make a note to myself in my Day-Timer to make sure my miles are registered when I check in at the gate. If they're not, I have my frequent flyer numbers for each airline I use in my address and phone directory to give to the agent. I don't have to wait while she looks up my account. ("Gee, the computers are sure slow today.") And I don't have to write any follow-up letters.

Prepare and save money

Here's another example. Between my office and my home, we have seven different printers for various computers that I use in my business and the kids use at home. Each printer has a different printer cartridge. (Why can't all the printer companies agree on a standard and make a universal cartridge that works in all printers? But, then again, I am the guy who still asks, "Why can't all music be recorded in the eight-track format?") I have a list of all the cartridge numbers in my address and phone directory. Then, if I am at the office supply store and they happen to have a special "two-for-one" sale of certain printer cartridges I can check to see if the ones I need are one sale and take advantage of the savings. A little preparation allows us to strike while the iron is hot.

Improving the job each day

IN CHAPTER 19 *I'll tell you how you can create about 2,500 little improvements in your life in one year, just by investing 10 minutes a day. But for now, think about one little improvement you can make in your job. Maybe you can move the fax machine closer to your desk (or farther away!) or make sure you have adequate supplies for the coming week, for example. Can you come up with one little improvement in your job that will increase your productivity? Sure, if you think about it. One little improvement does not sound like a lot because it isn't a lot. But great increases in your productivity don't necessarily require great increases in effort.*

Your "job" refers to more than just what you are paid to do. You and I have lots of jobs. You may have a job as an employee, a spouse, a friend, a parent, a neighbor, and so on. Wouldn't you be more efficient in all of your jobs if you made one little improvement to each?

■ **Making even the smallest changes** *in your life, such as spending more time with your family, can make all the difference.*

How small improvements can lead to great success

At a horserace, let's say the winner receives a $50,000 purse and the second-place horse receives a $25,000 purse. Why do we pay the first horse twice as much as the second horse? Does the first horse have to run twice as fast as the second horse to receive twice the reward? Of course not. The first horse only has to be a nose ahead of the second horse to enjoy twice the prize money.

That is a useful metaphor to keep in your mind about your own success. Great increases in your success do not necessarily require great increases in effort. Little improvements, done consistently over time, give you the accumulated benefit and can make a huge difference in your overall organization and productivity.

A portable file cabinet

I CARRY SOME OTHER USEFUL STUFF in my Day-Timer. I carry blank checks so I don't have to lug around my checkbook. I also carry a small amount of cash ($50) as emergency or mad money. I carry a couple of credit cards. I carry a separate wallet, which contains the usual wallet stuff, money, credit cards, pictures of my family, driver's license, etc. I don't like to combine all the wallet items with my Day-Timer because if I were to lose it, I would lose everything. By carrying a Day-Timer and a wallet, if I lose one, I have the other.

How you can keep track

When you go to the dry cleaners and receive the claim slip for your order, paper-clip it to the day you will be back to pick up your clothing. This is a lot better than having this claim slip in the visor of your car, where you might not notice it. If you have tickets to a sporting event or the theater, those are typically small enough that you can paper-clip them into your Day-Timer on the day you will use them. This way, you're not caught up at the last moment trying to remember what you did with the tickets. You can use your Day-Timer not only as a way of keeping track of appointments, scheduled events, and your to-do list, but also as a file cabinet of sorts.

■ **Just as you would file** *papers away in your desk, so you can use your Day-Timer as a portable filing system.*

Treat your Day-Timer with as much care as you would your wallet. If you're at a restaurant and you get up to go to the salad bar, you would not leave your wallet on your table, would you? I hope not. Don't leave your Day-Timer either. Treat it with the same respect to avoid losing it.

STEP 7:
START USING THESE USEFUL TOOLS

Commit right now to using the tools that have been presented to you in this chapter. Get a supply of 3 x 5 index cards and use them to get down on paper all those little things that slip through the cracks. Make up birthday, anniversary and gift-giving lists so you're always prepared. Assemble your telephone directory. Now you're really getting organized!

A simple summary

✔ Using 3 x 5 index cards will help you catch all the details that often slip through the cracks.

✔ An irritations list will help you catalog and reduce the little irritations that you can fix.

✔ A birthday and anniversary list is a good way to keep track of those important dates, while Christmas and birthday gift lists can help you develop your shopping lists in advance.

✔ Think of your small address and phone directory as your flat Rolodex.

✔ Improving the job each day with a single small improvement will yield major improvements in your life.

✔ In addition to keeping track of appointments and to-do items, you can use your Day-Timer like a portable file cabinet to store all kinds of information.

✔ Step 7 for organizing your life is to start using these useful tools.

Chapter 8

Overcoming Procrastination

Apopular phrase goes, "Why do today what you can put off until tomorrow?" You are doing all this daily planning and thinking and writing about what you will do, but what if you don't take action? What if you procrastinate? If you have too much to do, it's easy to tell yourself you'll worry about getting it done tomorrow. You need some tools and techniques to overcome procrastination, and that's what I'll share with you in this chapter.

In this chapter...

✓ Why we procrastinate

✓ Pain and pleasure is what motivates us

✓ Conquering procrastination

✓ Step 8: List your procrastinated items and solutions

WHO WOULDN'T RATHER LINGER IN THE PARK THAN FACE A MOUND OF PAPERWORK?

Why we procrastinate

WHY DO WE PROCRASTINATE and put off the crucial and important things we know we need to do? There are several reasons. Sometimes it's fear of the unknown. If we've never attempted the task before we may not know how to do it. Sometimes it's because we're afraid of failing. Other times it's unpleasant or just plain difficult to do a task, and we naturally shy away from unpleasantness and put off things that are difficult. Perhaps we don't have enough information to proceed, or we don't know how to proceed. Occasionally, it's plain old laziness that makes us procrastinate.

> **DEFINITION**
>
> **Procrastination** is the practice of postponing today what you know you ought to be doing to a time in the future when you are likely to feel the same way.

■ **There will always be** *a thousand things you'd much rather do than write that report, make that call, or prepare for that meeting.*

Don't put off crucial and important tasks

Procrastination serves a useful purpose when we put off C and D items, the things that have little or no value. Putting off C and D items may give you more time for the A and B items in your day, so it's probably a good idea to develop ways to procrastinate those C and D items. The problem is, many of us put off A and B tasks, the ones that are crucial and important.

You must get round to it!

There are two reasons why you should not put off doing the A and B tasks in your day:

1 You reduce your productivity. You are not getting done what you know you need to get done. Your success is therefore diminished.

2 You are increasing your stress because you know you should be completing these important items that you are putting off.

From there it has a snowball effect. When you are stressed because you are procrastinating, that affects the next thing that you do, perhaps a phone call to a customer. Your voice is not quite relaxed and the result is less than satisfactory. You are a little angry with yourself as a result of how the phone call went. You now move on to the next thing you must deal with, perhaps a meeting with someone. Still stressed and a bit angry, you're a little short with this person and the result of your meeting is less than you desired. Now you feel guilty over how you treated that person.

INTERNET

www.carleton.ca/ ~tpychyl/

Carleton University in Ottawa, Canada, maintains this site as the Procrastination Research Group. It's a compilation of information and research on procrastination from all over the world.

So now you are stressed, angry, and guilty. (Sounds like a law firm, doesn't it?) This affects the next thing you must do. Get the point? I may be exaggerating here a bit, but I'm sure you see how the original procrastination cycles itself in the wrong direction, accumulating related negative emotions and hurting your productivity.

■ **Putting off difficult** *or awkward tasks can have a negative effect on those around you, and provoke a stressful situation.*

Pain and pleasure is what motivates us

IT'S IMPORTANT TO UNDERSTAND why something is happening, because if you know why something is occurring you are in a much better position to control and prevent it.

All of our decisions to act or not to act are controlled by pain and pleasure. We naturally avoid pain and we naturally seek out pleasure. This is part of the survival instinct. If there is no pain for not doing something and no pleasure to do the same task, we do not act. We are immobilized.

■ **Why is it that** *when you are busiest, the people around you always seem to be doing something far more interesting that distracts you from what you should be doing?*

■ **Don't be distracted** *when you have a deadline to meet. Give yourself something pleasurable to look forward to when you've finished the job – a date with good friends, for example.*

Let's say you get home around 6 p.m. tonight. You feel hunger pains, so what do you do? You have something to eat. Why? To alleviate the hunger pains. You may continue to eat even when you have no more hunger pains. Why do you do that? Pleasure. You like those cookies. However, if you have no hunger pains and there is food in front of you that you don't care for, you will probably not eat it.

Avoiding pain and seeking pleasure

As another example, let's say you are a student in my business law class. It's the first day of the new term and I am telling you that in order to successfully pass this course you must, in addition to all other tests and assignments, submit by the last day of class, a 40-page, single-spaced, typewritten term paper, with footnotes and bibliography, on some obscure topic such as "The Latest Developments in Global Legal Systems from 1902–1909." That's a pretty unattractive assignment!

The term begins on February 1 and ends on May 15. Would you go home tonight, on February 1, the first day of class, and start working on this term paper? Probably not. Some would, but most wouldn't. Why? Because there is probably little pleasure associated with doing this assignment, and many would agree, a lot of pain to complete it. So what do you do? You procrastinate.

Let us push the calendar ahead a bit. It is now May 13, 2 days before the end of the term and the deadline for submitting the term paper. You still have not started work on the paper. Do you rush home tonight and begin? Many would respond with a resounding "Yes!" But if you're a real procrastinator, you'll think, why do the paper tonight when I still have 2 more days?

Is there any more pleasure associated with doing the term paper May 13 than earlier in the term? Not really. In fact, there's a lot of satisfaction in doing the paper early in the term and knowing you've completed it, especially if other students are feeling their stress levels rise as the deadline looms. But there is a big pain coming your way if you do not complete it within 2 days. It's called failing the class and having to repeat it. To avoid the higher pain of failing the class, you now submit yourself to doing what you could have done a long time ago. If you understand how this works – that we are motivated by avoiding pain and seeking pleasure – you can now get a handle on your procrastination.

■ **You can avoid** *becoming a victim of procrastination by getting started on jobs well ahead of time;.this will save you unnecessary worry – and sleepless nights.*

Avoid putting yourself through the stress that procrastination creates. The price is not worth it. It impacts on other things in your life.

It's a state of mind

If you want to control procrastination, you either have to create enough pain in your mind from not doing the task, or create in your mind enough pleasure to do it. Which way sounds more effective to you?

When I was growing up, I had to wash the family dishes from time to time. Many of my friends did too, but a lot of them approached this task in misery. They did it out of pain avoidance. They did it to avoid punishment. As a result, they would spend 15 or 20 minutes in discomfort, not because of what they had to do but because of the way they were approaching the task. I, on the other hand, would always approach unpleasant tasks like washing dishes from the standpoint of pleasure. It didn't mean I was better than some of my friends. I just looked at the task differently. I grew up in the 1950s during the Cold War. I would start washing dishes around 6:40 p.m. and would tell myself, "If these dishes are completely done by 7 p.m., the world will not blow up in a nuclear war!"

Kind of silly, I know. But you know what? I was not just washing dishes any more. I was saving the world! Did I get grease and soap all over me? Sure. But what a small price to pay to save humanity! And the time would go by real fast and it wasn't such a bad thing. Then, the next time I had to wash the dishes, I would change the rules. I would tell myself that I had to beat my previous record of 20 minutes. And after a few days, I would change the entire game.

■ **We've all been there** – *the staring into space, feeling lethargic and unmotivated. The best way to avoid these symptoms of procrastination is to change your attitude about the job you have to do.*

We all have it in us to be creative enough to take an unpleasant or difficult task, one that we are putting off, and look at it in a different light so that it becomes a pleasurable task. If we can do this, we can get a handle on our procrastination.

Conquering procrastination

HERE ARE FIVE *useful techniques you can use to help overcome procrastination and get going on the things you should be doing.*

1.) Do your daily planning

More than anything else, daily planning will move you out of inaction and into action that will help enhance your productivity. "Plan your work and work your plan." This is important in both your work and personal life. Without a plan of action we tend to respond to the easier tasks or the ones that are screaming for our attention, but this may not be the best use of our time.

For example, let's say that this evening I need to read a chapter in a new business book I just purchased, and I would like to do some work on my computer. I have not planned these activities and put them on my to-do list for tonight. Here's what happens.

■ **Everyone knows** *that no matter how long you put off doing something it will still be there, waiting to be done, and loom even larger in your mind the more you avoid it.*

I get home around 6 p.m. and there's a newspaper on the counter. What do I do with it? I read it. Why pay for a subscription and not read it? Plus, I need to know what is going on in this world. It takes some time. It is now 6:45 p.m. I'm hungry, so I eat something. Then I wash the dirty dishes and spend some time cleaning up the kitchen. It is now 7:15 p.m. and I haven't done what I need to do.

The phone rings and I answer it. It could be important, although it almost never is. Sure enough, it's someone trying to sell me his product or service. I am not critical of these people. If I were in their business, I would probably try to sell the way they sell. The point is, this is keeping me from doing what I really need to do, which is read that chapter in my new business book and do some work on my computer. It is now 7:25 p.m. and it occurs to me that tonight, THE GAME is on television. I am entitled to watch the game. After all, I've had a tough day and everyone will be talking about it tomorrow at work. So I watch the game.

■ **Everyone knows it's impossible** *to work when you're hungry. How are you possibly going to be able to concentrate if you don't eat first?*

It is now 9:35 p.m., I have watched the game but I have not read my book or worked on the computer. I am just about to when my son comes home from his basketball tryouts and we chat about that for a while. It is now 10:10 p.m. and the phone rings again. It's my sister calling from California to chat. We have not chatted for over a month and the next thing I know, it's 10:55 p.m. when I hang up the phone. Time for bed!

■ **A classic avoidance tactic** *is to do everything else possible that you can think of before getting around to what you know you should be doing.*

I did not get my chapter read. I did not work on my computer. Why? Because I met face to face with one of the largest enemies to personal productivity: I got caught up in stuff. It's easy to get caught up in stuff both at home and at work. Stuff is always there to occupy our time. The antidote is to plan your work and personal time for each day when you make up your to-do list the night before. As I've said, there is only one way to get time – you have to take it.

If we could get to the bottom of the bucket of stuff and be done with it so we could move on to doing the truly important things, that would be great. But the truth is, there is always more stuff that occupies our time and keeps us from doing the things that will enhance our success.

2.) Tackle one part at a time

How do you eat an elephant? The answer is, one bite at a time. If I have a large project to work on that will take, say, 3 hours to complete and I schedule it as my A-1 task for the next day, I am likely to procrastinate. For one thing, I rarely get a solid block of 3 hours to work on any one task. I don't know if I even have an attention span that lasts 3 hours. But I fool myself into thinking that tomorrow will be different from the reality of the past, and I put that entire 3-hour project on my to-do list as an A-1. Of course, at the end of the day, I have not still completed it and am feeling stressed out.

Rather than put the entire project down, a better approach is to divide it into steps, which I schedule on my to-do list over the next several days. I put down the first step, which might take me 15 to 20 minutes. I can get 15 to 20 minutes. I accomplish this first bite of the elephant and then I put the next bite on the to-do list for the following day. It might take me several days, a bite a day, but I will get that big elephant eaten up.

■ **You will actually** *cause yourself more stress by playing the avoidance game than if you faced up to what has to be done.*

3.) Schedule it up front

Ever notice when people eat a piece of pie they will typically start at the pointy end, eat the good stuff first and save the crust until last? This is generally true because most find the crust is the less desirable part of the pie.

The point is this: If you have something unpleasant to do – a difficult phone call to make, for example – and you schedule it for late in the day, you give yourself all day to think up reasons why maybe tomorrow is a better time to make the call and you will have successfully put off making it. Schedule the unpleasant tasks up front, first thing in your day. Get them done and out of the way. That way, you will not have the rest of the day to think up reasons to procrastinate.

■ **Take the bull** *by the horns and deal with an unpleasant task early in the day. This achievement will give you a huge boost.*

4.) Set a deadline

Have you ever established a New Year's resolution that you did not follow through on? We are often truly motivated on January 1. "This is the year I will stop smoking." "This is the year I will lose weight." Then, 12 months later, on December 31, most have not accomplished their goal. Why? Because they did not have a deadline. Deadlines move us to action. Without them, responsibilities tend to wind up in the "as-soon-as-possible" pile because we all have too much to do.

■ **If you have something** *pleasurable to look forward to – spending your summer vacation at the beach, for example – you will find it much easier to stick to your New Year's resolution of getting into shape.*

SETTING A DEADLINE

How do we create deadlines? Here are three ways for you to remember:

1 You are given a deadline. "Susan, here is the Smith report. I will need this completed by Thursday at 2 p.m." That's clear, and chances are good that Susan will have the report done by Thursday at 2 p.m.

2 You ask for the deadline. Occasionally people request our help and ask that we get something done "as soon as possible." The problem is that people interpret "as soon as possible" differently. I may think as soon as possible means one week from now. The person giving me the assignment may think it means tomorrow. Now we have set the stage for unnecessary friction between us.

3 You establish the deadline. "I will have this done for you by Tuesday at 3 p.m."

■ **Rather than creating stress,** *deadlines increase productivity immeasurably. If you have a deadline, work with that date in mind, and get the job done on time.*

If you're unclear about a deadline, ask. Use the correct question, though, which is, "When do you need it?" Often, many people will ask the wrong question, which is, "When do you want it?" Most people will say they want something a lot sooner than they may need it.

Trivia...

According to a recent study conducted by USA Today, by January 31 of each year, 66 percent of all New Year's resolutions have already been abandoned.

5.) Just get going on it!

When I was attending law school, I would come home at night with a hundred or more pages of text to read as homework. It was long, tedious stuff. There were no pictures. I would open the book to the first page of the assignment and tell myself I would read the first page only. That would only take 5 minutes and then I could go off and watch television or engage in other more pleasurable pursuits. There was a convoluted logic in all of this. I could report to my professor the next day that I had read the material. Of course, I would not have read it all.

■ **You know you should** *get started on your reading, but surely five more minutes and another cup of coffee will keep you in the right frame of mind, right? Don't you believe it!*

But I found what invariably happened is that the next thing I knew I was finishing up the last pages of the entire assignment. There is just something about getting started. Start something and in all likelihood, it will take on a life of its own to get you to completion.

Remember as a kid if you went to the lake or shore at the beginning of the summer to take a dip, there were two ways to get into the water? First there was the torture method when you put in a toe, shivered, and convinced yourself it was too cold and you procrastinated getting in at all. The second method was to jump in or maybe get pushed in. After a few minutes of shivering, you became acclimated and enjoyed the water. It's the same thing with procrastination. Sometimes you have to just jump right in.

Have you ever procrastinated cleaning out a garage or a closet? Don't tell yourself that you are going to clean out the entire closet. Just tell yourself you are going to organize the blouses. That should only take 10 minutes. Just getting started on a task will often get you beyond your procrastination.

■ **Take the plunge** – *if you don't get started, you'll never get anything done.*

STEP 8:
LIST YOUR PROCRASTINATED ITEMS
AND SOLUTIONS

Review the items on your to-do list that you have been carrying forward, that you have been procrastinating about doing. Use the tools in this chapter to get each one done.

■ **Begin your procrastination-free life** *by tackling something that will provide immediate results. This success will put you in the right frame of mind to organize other aspects of your life.*

A simple summary

✔ We procrastinate for many reasons, including fear of failure and laziness.

✔ Procrastinating non-crucial tasks is okay because it gives you more time for the crucial and important tasks.

✔ Pain and pleasure is what motivates us away from or into action.

✔ Five tips can help you conquer procrastination and keep you organized and productive.

✔ Procrastination is all about your state of mind, so try and change the way you view tasks.

✔ Step 8 for organizing your life is to list your procrastinated items and solutions.

Chapter 9

The Importance of Delegation

DOESN'T IT OFTEN SEEM like there's not enough time in the day to get everything done? We all have 24 hours in each day and 7 days in each week, and while the quantity of time we get is fixed, we can achieve the same result through the time of others as we delegate. Delegating tasks is the key to opening up the door to expanded success in our lives. This chapter is all about what delegating can do for you.

In this chapter...

✓ Plugging into someone else's time stream

✓ You already delegate a lot

✓ The hardest part about delegating

✓ Use networking for more results

✓ Step 9: Decide what tasks you could have delegated to others

DELEGATE YOUR GROCERY SHOPPING IN RETURN FOR SOME QUALITY FAMILY TIME

Plugging into someone else's time stream

DEFINITION

Delegation is the practice of assigning tasks to others. In doing so you leverage your time and multiply your success.

I DO A LOT OF ONE-ON-ONE coaching with business executives who want to improve their organizational and time-management skills. Almost always, I find that executives who put in an extraordinary number of hours and face potential burnout have a problem with **delegation.** *They cannot let go and let others do what needs to be done. So they are there first thing in the morning and last thing at night, putting in those extra hours unnecessarily and adversely impacting their personal balance.*

Some people get an exaggerated sense about their own importance. They feel "the place would fall apart" if they were not there to handle every detail that comes along. They feel they are indispensable to the success of the operation. I must admit that I too sometimes fall into this trap. I think I am very good at what I do, presenting my time management seminars and writing extensively about it. But if I were to die tonight, would there be someone out there who could take my place and teach and write as well as I do? Of course – and not only as well as I do it, but probably better.

This is not to diminish our importance or the value of what we do. Sure, we are all important and make valuable contributions. But for whatever reason, if we were no longer present, the world would go on. We do not have to die to prove the point.

Cemeteries are filled with "indispensable" people. No one is truly indispensable; we will all have a last day.

■ **Avoid burn-out at work,** *and be pleasantly surprised by how much your attitude changes by delegating tasks to others. Don't assume that no one else can do the job as well as you can.*

You already delegate a lot

SOME PEOPLE FEEL they are not in a position to delegate and have no one to delegate to. The fact is, you already delegate a lot; you just don't realize it.

Unconscious delegation

Let's say you visit the department store and purchase a cotton shirt for $30. Could you have created that shirt on your own, from scratch? Sure, not that you would have desired to spend your time in that way. To create that shirt from scratch, you would have to plant a cottonseed, harvest the mature cotton balls, and process them into material. You would then have to create a pattern and tools like a sewing needle to put it all together. You could have done all that and spent maybe hundreds of hours of your time accomplish this, but instead you made an unconscious decision that this was not the best use of your time. So you journey down to the department store, give them $30, and walk out with your new shirt.

Is this an example of delegation? Of course. Delegation is when you plug into someone else's time stream when you don't have the time or expertise to do something yourself. The clothing manufacturer and all who were involved in the production of your shirt created a benefit to you through the time of others.

■ **Even the simple act** *of buying a shirt entails delegation. Instead of making the shirt yourself, you have used the services of the manufacturers.*

What we get from delegating

Do you have mail delivered to your home? Most people do. As an alternative, could you rent a post office box at your local post office and drive your car there each day to retrieve your mail? Sure, but most of us prefer to have the letter carrier deliver our mail to us. Perhaps you have your newspaper delivered to your house each day instead of going to the store to pick it up.

Did you go out for lunch recently? Perhaps you got a hamburger, fries, and a drink for lunch and paid $5 for the meal. How many people were involved in the preparation of that meal? Hundreds, and maybe more. Someone had to plant the potato seed for the fries, pick the tomatoes off the vine to create the catsup, and drill the oil out of the ground to fuel the truck's trip from the meat-packing plant to your local restaurant. And if you paid $5 for this meal, didn't everyone in this chain have to share in that economic reward, that $5? Yes, they did, perhaps in fractions of a penny each.

■ **Every time you go out for a meal** *you are delegating a whole series of tasks to others – everything from actually growing the food to preparing it and putting it on the table.*

I am not trying to get silly about this idea of delegation and stretch it to some unrealistic point. This is exactly the way the world worked up until a couple of hundred years ago. If you wanted almost anything, you had to create it yourself. If you were hungry, you didn't visit your local fast-food restaurant. They did not exist. You had to grow your own food or catch it yourself. If you wanted clothing, you didn't drive to your local department store. You had to make it yourself. If you wanted housing, you didn't visit your local real estate agent, look at a variety of pictures, and then decide on your new residence. You had to clear the land yourself and build your own housing.

■ **The Industrial Revolution** *meant that individuals no longer had to do everything for themselves; as a result, there can be a host of people responsible for making most of the things we now take for granted.*

Personal wealth

And if we examine the development of individual personal wealth from whenever it started to be tracked up until a couple of hundred years ago, it did not go up much over time. People a couple of hundred years ago were not a whole better off financially than any of their ancestors.

Then about 200 years ago came the Industrial Revolution. The concept of mechanized manufacturing processes permitted companies to put out great quantities of products at relative low cost, which required companies to pay relatively good wages so workers could afford to purchase these products. As a result, individual personal wealth has shot up through the roof to where it is today.

The Industrial Revolution started in England around 1760 with the first cotton mill. It marks a time when our economic focus moved away from farming to manufacturing.

What we'd have without it

If we had to do everything ourselves, provide for our food, shelter, clothing, medical care, and luxuries, we would have but a tiny fraction of what we have now. It would vary from person to person, but I would suggest that 95 percent of what you have now as results in any of your seven vital areas is coming to you through the help of others, through delegation. Or the flip side, if you had do everything yourself, you would probably have just 5 percent or less of what you have already.

So, the issue is not whether you use delegation. You do, in a variety of ways you perhaps didn't recognize. The real question is, how far do you want to go with it? Delegation is the tool to provide you with great increases in your personal productivity because you are limited in the time you have available.

The hardest part about delegating

THE HARDEST PART ABOUT DELEGATING *is not finding ways to do it effectively, as we will discuss in Chapter 10, but just letting go. We take great pride in doing things ourselves. "If you want a job done right, you have to do it yourself," is the motto of many people.*

■ **You must learn** *to let go and delegate; it is not true that only you can do a job right.*

■ **Have your kids** *prepare their own picnic – this will not only give you some more free time, but will teach them some useful lessons, too.*

My wife and I have had this discussion over the years. When our four children were all at home, my wife would do all the laundry in addition to many other tasks. Doing the laundry for 6 people is a big job. Sometimes she would say she wished she had more time for gardening, and yet she would always put in a few hours each day doing the laundry. I suggested she delegate this task to the kids. (If I was really a nice guy, I guess I would have volunteered to do it myself.) Sure, the kids! Ten- and 11-year-olds can be taught to do laundry, and it would free my wife to use her time in other ways – maybe even some of that gardening she wanted to do.

My wife's response was always the same: "By the time I show them how to do it, I could have just as quickly done it myself." Have you ever said that? It's a trap, isn't it? As the saying goes, "If you give a man a fish, he feeds himself for a day. But if you teach a man how to fish, he can feed himself for a lifetime."

A stitch in time

You see, this is the difference between expensing or spending time and investing time, which I first mentioned in Chapter 1. You don't have to be math major to appreciate that it makes little sense to spend an hour to teach someone how to do a 10-minute task. But when you realize that 1-hour investment will save you 10 minutes a day, each and every day, in less than a week you get your investment back and it continues to pay dividends well into the future. Good time managers are not concerned with how much time something takes. They want to know what are they getting back for the time they invest. Good time managers are good investors.

Don't focus on how much time something takes. Focus instead on what you get back from investing that time.

Going back to my wife and the laundry, she would then raise the issue that while she could, indeed, invest the time to teach the kids how to do the laundry, they would still make mistakes in the process. They might put the red jeans in with the white T-shirts and the T-shirts would come out of the wash pink. My reaction to that was, "So what?" What's wrong with pink T-shirts? I think they are attractive!" Not very helpful.

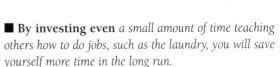

■ **By investing even** *a small amount of time teaching others how to do jobs, such as the laundry, you will save yourself more time in the long run.*

Can you imagine a universal rule that says no child can make a peanut-butter sandwich until they know how to make a peanut-butter sandwich? That would be a dumb rule. Do you remember the first time your 2-year-old child or relative made her first peanut-butter sandwich? It was not exactly a 5-star gourmet delight. Peanut butter was everywhere. There was a mess to clean up. But don't you agree that some of these 2-year-olds will become chefs in major hotels one day? They are going to have to go through hundreds of peanut-butter sandwiches to get there. It's part of the learning process.

Learning the hard way

We all learn through our failures. Failure is a good teacher. In professional baseball, when you get up to bat, if you miss seven times out of ten, you are a good candidate for their Hall of Fame. How did you learn to do what you do so well except through failure?

There is a lot of difference between, "I do it" and "It gets done." Which is more important? It gets done. It's great that you can and want to do a variety of things, but remember, you have a limited number of hours available each week and you have to be careful how you spend them.

As you delegate to others, be careful not to micro-manage what you have delegated to ensure the proper result. Many people delegate in this manner and then complain that delegation does not work because they have to spend the same amount of time making sure it gets done correctly.

■ **Everyone,** *including professionals, has made mistakes — and learned from them.*

Use networking for more results

AN IMPORTANT TECHNIQUE for delegating tasks is to develop a network of people you trust and can rely on. I started this process when I was in college. Whenever I would meet people, I recorded their information on an index card. This included fellow students and my professors – anyone who, if I telephoned them and they heard it was me calling, would take my call. That was the only criteria for being included in my list. Today, that database is on my computer and includes contact information for over 4,000 people.

Trivia...
I went from recording networking data on paper years ago to recording this data in my computer. The software I use allows me to not only keep track of contact information such as names, addresses, and telephone numbers, it also permits me to categorize people by their interests and occupations. This way I can quickly identify all the accountants on my list or all of those who enjoy tennis.

■ **Build up a network of people** *you can turn to – people who have helped you in the past, or who have just listened.*

Keep in touch

For this contact list to be of value, it is not enough to meet someone, put their name on your list, and then ask for something from them when you are in need. If you want to have a friend, you have to be a friend. Politicians are good at this. Members of the United States House of Representatives are elected for 2-year terms. More than 95 percent who seek re-election get re-elected. As soon as they are elected, they place a high priority on constituent services. Are you having trouble getting your Social Security check? Do you need some information about a scholarship program funded by the federal government? Call your congressman. If he is worth his salt and is doing his job, he will get you what you need and solidify his bond with you. If he does a good enough job, you might even tell a friend or two. Then come re-election time, your congressman needs something from you, your vote. Having done a good job for you, you may be inclined to give it. Do you want to be an effective networker? Be a good politician first.

■ **When you meet** *someone in your field, don't forget to exchange phone numbers or business cards; you never know when you might need their help – or their contacts.*

A friend in need . . .

I spend a lot of my time serving my network first. I am always clipping out newspaper articles and sending them to people I know may be interested. I send a lot of birthday cards, I call people now and again, not to get something, but to remind them that if they need help, I am here for them.

Finally, delegation is not dumping something on another just to get it off your plate. Delegation is giving it to the right person, and making sure the person has the information, the tools, and the authority to do what you are asking. Delegation also requires giving others the authority to make some decisions. We often get hung up on a certain way of doing things. In truth, there really is no one way of doing anything. There is "my way" and "your way," and there may always be a better way.

The more you delegate, the better people will get at handling those responsibilities. People around you will tend to rise to your level of expectation for them, and they will sink to your low level of expectation for them as well. If you keep telling those around you, "This is a real important customer, better let me handle this" or "Better let Mommy do this," you will send a message of incompetence to those around you that they will probably buy into. But if you delegate and encourage those around you to take on more tasks, they will rise in their abilities.

■ **If you need a little free time** *to get things done, why not ask a member of your family to help you out for a few hours?*

STEP 9:
DECIDE WHAT TASKS YOU COULD HAVE DELEGATED TO OTHERS

Review what you have done in the last couple of weeks and determine which items you could have delegated to others that would have freed up your time for more important matters.

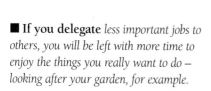

■ **If you delegate** *less important jobs to others, you will be left with more time to enjoy the things you really want to do — looking after your garden, for example.*

A simple summary

✔ Plugging into someone else's time stream by delegating tasks will leverage your success.

✔ You already delegate a lot. Perhaps 95 percent of what you have now comes to you from delegation, although you may not realize it.

✔ The hardest part of delegation is just letting go.

✔ It may seem quicker to do something yourself, but in the long run to teach someone else to do it will save you time.

✔ Use networking for more results by keeping track of the people you meet.

✔ Step 9 for organizing your life is to decide what tasks you could have delegated to others.

Chapter 10

Specific Ways to Delegate

DELEGATION IS ALL ABOUT plugging into someone else's time stream when we do not have the time or the expertise to do something. Delegation doesn't mean taking advantage of someone else's resources, but should be a fair transaction for all. And with over 6 billion people on the planet, there are plenty of people to help us multiply our results. In this chapter I'll show you the techniques for effective delegating.

In this chapter...

✓ Delegating to staff: ask and you may receive

✓ Reverse delegation

✓ Your inner circle

✓ College "gophers"

✓ Hiring some extra help

✓ Step 10: Decide what and to whom you can delegate

159

Delegating to staff: ask and you may receive

WHEN DECIDING WHO *to delegate to, consider staff members first. Current management philosophy suggests that you push decision making to the lowest level. Get as many people involved because what they write, they will underwrite.*

Sharing the burden

Now you might be sitting there saying, "I am the staff. I have no staff person to delegate to!" The idea of delegating to a staff person may not be an appropriate suggestion for all readers. But wait a minute. If you know that having a staff person can help in some measure to alleviate your time-management crunch and you do not have a staff person to delegate to, why not think about ways to get one?

A student in one of my time-management seminars worked as an engineer for a large corporation. He was overloaded with work. Like many of us when we have a time-management challenge, we pay for it out of our hides and put in more time. This was how he was responding to his predicament. He was putting in more time, nights, and weekends – so much so that he was getting out of balance, especially in the family area, which is why he wound up in my time-management seminar in the first place.

■ **All of us get** *overloaded at one time or another; under these circumstances it is vital to get assistance, rather than trying to "do it all" yourself.*

> ### Trivia...
> *Each night in daily planning, I review all my to-do list items, appointments, and scheduled events. As I review each I ask, "Is this the best use of my time?" If it is, I plan to personally attend to the task. If not, I try to think of a way to delegate it to a staff member.*

One of the suggestions he liked was the idea of working with a clean desk (which we'll discuss in Chapter 12). He was living with a swirling pile of papers all around him, all screaming for his attention. He took control of that situation, cleaned up the messy desk and discovered that he had about 12 weeks' worth of work and only 6 weeks' worth of deadlines. He was overcommitted two to one. This happens to a lot of people. On the one hand, we are trained to say "yes" when someone asks for our help. On the other hand, many of us do not have an adequate measuring stick to see how far in we are, and the next thing you know you are in over your head, drowning in overcommitments and paying for it with more and more time.

Don't ask, won't get

I asked him what he thought the solution was. He said, "If I could hire a junior-level engineer, I could assign much of this workload to that person and get all this done within the deadlines." "Good," I replied. "Now that you have your solution, when will you implement it?" "You don't understand," he went on. "I am the staff. I have no authority to hire anyone." I replied, "Well, if you don't have the authority, who does?"

Someone can authorize anything in this world. All things are possible. The Bible says "Ask and ye shall receive"; it does not say, "Sit there and think about it. Maybe it will come your way." So ask. This is one of the most powerful time-management tools you have available to you.

If you ask for something and are turned down, you lose nothing. Ask anyway. The result may surprise you. My student decided to go to the person with authority, his boss, and ask if a junior engineer could be hired to assist him. His request was granted and the company was able to hire a staff person for my friend, helping him solve his time-management issue.

Now I understand the real world. I am not suggesting that if you go to the authorities in your company and say, "Dr. Wetmore says I am entitled to an assistant," you will get one. I understand about budgets and hiring freezes. All I am suggesting is that you owe it to yourself to ask. Even if you are turned down you will feel better about the issue, because at least you tried. Knowing is a whole lot better than not knowing. What if my student had been turned down in his request for a staff person? He could apply the technique of reverse delegation.

■ **Instead of drowning** *in work, ask your superiors to hire some help; even if they don't deliver, at least you will have tried to resolve the problem.*

Reverse delegation

REVERSE DELEGATION *is when you "undo" a delegation or a potential delegation to you using one of two questions, "Which do you want back?" or "What do you think?" "Which do you want back?" is a way of returning some of your responsibilities to the person who gave them to you in the first place when you find you are overcommitted and unable to ever complete them. The "What do you think?" question is an effective way of helping the person who is trying to give something to you find the solution they were looking to you for in the first place.*

■ **If you have been given** *too much work, use reverse delegation to decide how to prioritize tasks.*

Renegotiating

If my student's request for an assistant had been turned down, with 12 weeks' worth of work and only 6 weeks' worth of deadline, he could go to his boss and, referring to his list of tasks, ask, "Which do you want back?" It's a fair question. You are entitled to ask it. Or, you might ask, "Which of these tasks can I renegotiate the deadline for so that I have 12 weeks of deadline with 12 weeks of work?"

I believe in working hard. I work as hard as almost anyone I know. I believe that we ought to give a good day's work for a good day's pay. Hard work and loyalty are good things. Approximately one-third of the work force changes jobs each year and one of the major causes for job change is stress and job burn-out. If we find ourselves in a situation that may eventually lead us to burning out and leaving our organization, what good are we then to the organization when we are gone?

■ **Although it's flattering** *when colleagues ask for your advice, make sure that you don't become too involved in other peoples' work when you are stretched to the limit yourself.*

When dedication to hard work and loyalty is pushed beyond reasonable capacity to a point where you may be burning yourself out, it becomes self-defeating.

The second question of the reverse delegation technique is using the question, "What do you think?" I have several people, staff, students, friends, and family approach me from time to time to ask for help or advice. Whenever someone is asking for my input, I am flattered. I take it as a real compliment that someone would think enough of my opinion or knowledge to ask for it. The problem is, I sometimes then get embroiled in their issues and have little or no time to do what I need to do.

Helping others to help themselves

For example, my office manager came to me one day all stressed out. "The ABC Company wants to book a seminar with you for the first week in April, but the XYZ wants you for the same week and I don't know what to do!" she exclaimed. Whenever anyone approaches me in that fashion, my reaction is typically, "Okay, give this to me and I will take care of it." My office manager would gladly hand the problem over to me and leave the room with a smile on her face. If this happened a few more times in my day, I could easily get buried in the problems of others.

Instead, I used reverse delegation and asked my office manager, "What do you think?" She replied, "Well, I guess I could move ABC over to the time slot we have available in May. Or maybe I could schedule XYZ for later in the month." My reply was, "Good solutions. Let me know which one you select." She still had the problem when she walked out of my office, but now she was on her way to resolving the problem on her own – and that was one less problem for me to get bogged down in.

■ **If someone approaches** *you with a problem, instead of resolving it yourself, use reverse delegation so that they find their own solution.*

You may have no problem taking on your share of the load, but the person bringing you the problem is often just as well equipped to handle it as you are.

Ask the right question

In many cases you may be able to reverse-delegate a task back to someone before you get tied up in it by asking that person the question, "What do you think?" There is a very powerful word in that question. It is "you." That is a word of empowerment. "You have solved things like this before. What do you think?" "You" creates independence. Often we use a weaker word in our communications with others, and that is "I." "This is how I would do it." "This is what I think ought to be done." When you say "I" you send a message of dependence.

Most of the time when you use this approach, you'll find that the person who is bringing the situation to you is just as capable as you are of solving it and will arrive at a good solution by responding to this question.

Everything outlined in this book will not work 100 percent of the time, but if it works 20 percent or 50 percent of the time, you will have that much more time to do what you deem to be a more productive use of your time.

Your inner circle

YOUR SPOUSE, *your significant other, your children, your family, your friends, and your coworkers are all part of your inner circle. These are the people who are closest to you, who care for you the most, and who are most likely to help you if you ask.*

The best way to have a friend is to be a friend. If you offer something that is worth more than what you asking for in return, you will get what you need. For example, I could say to my wife, "I want you to drop off the shirts at the dry cleaners each week rather than me do it." It's a straightforward request and I may be able to delegate this task, but the relationship with my wife may be harmed in the process. A more effective approach might be, "You know how you wash your car every weekend and don't like doing it? I was wondering, how about if I wash your car each weekend and in return, maybe you could drop the shirts off at the cleaners each week?"

■ **Your friends and family** *can always be relied on to help you out — but only if you treat them as you would like to be treated!*

College "gophers"

WHAT IF YOU WERE *able to purchase an extra 10 or 20 hours per week to spend time with your family or develop that business on the side? Would that make a difference in your life?*

Each of us has 10 to 20 hours per week of small things that have to be done to make our lives run smoothly. We have to clean the house, wash our clothes, grocery shop, go to the pharmacy, and many other things. There is nothing wrong with you doing these things yourself. I know many couples who enjoy grocery shopping together on Saturdays because that is one of the few times during the week that they get to spend time together. But if you're finding you don't have enough time to do the things you really want to do, to realize your dreams and goals, and you are spending 10 to 20 hours per week doing this lower-level stuff, perhaps you have a choice. And the choice might be to hire a college assistant. The job title is affectionately called "gopher," as in "go for this and go for that." I recommend a college student rather than a high school student because you will typically get a more mature individual and will have greater flexibility in scheduling.

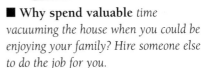

■ **Why spend valuable** *time vacuuming the house when you could be enjoying your family? Hire someone else to do the job for you.*

■ **You are bound** *to find someone at your local college who would be more than happy to make some money doing a variety of jobs around the house.*

Tasks for a gopher

To recruit someone, call the placement department at a few colleges in your immediate area and get their fax number. Prepare a job opening notice such as "College "Gopher" – Looking for responsible individual to do a variety of personal tasks including shopping, running errands, and cleaning. Must have own car and a good driving record. Flexible hours. $X.XX per hour. For an interview, please call xxx-xxx-xxxx."

Fax your ad to the various placement offices with a request that they post this job opening. You will get phone calls shortly and should be able to fill your position quickly. Then assign all those little tasks to this person and free up your time to do something that is more productive and fulfilling, like spending time with your family or developing hobbies. Let your gopher get the gas in the car, mow the lawn, dust and vacuum the house, run to the pharmacy, pick up the dry cleaning, do the laundry, and do the grocery shopping.

INTERNET

www.iavoa.com/

A whole new profession of virtual assistants is emerging to help you get more done in less time through delegation. Check out this web site, run by the International Association of Virtual Office Assistants (IAVOA), for a discussion on the benefits of using virtual assistants and a directory of its members.

By the way, the students who do this work usually love it, because the alternative is typically working in a closely supervised position at a fast-food restaurant or a factory. Those are not bad jobs, but being your gopher gives them a lot more freedom.

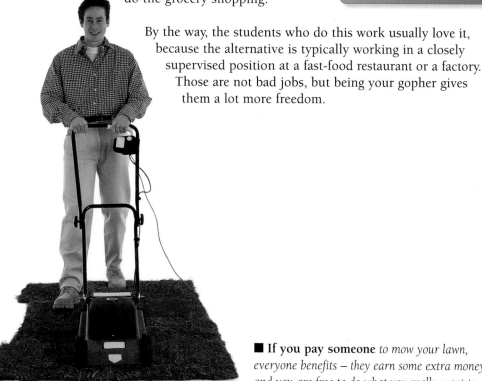

■ **If you pay someone** *to mow your lawn, everyone benefits – they earn some extra money and you are free to do what you really want to do.*

Hiring some extra help

A FINAL AREA to use delegation is in the area of hired help. It is similar to hiring a college assistant, only at the next level up. Hired help is available to do almost anything. Plumbers, electricians, lawn-care services, snow-plowing companies, auto mechanics, and house-cleaning services can help you get more time for the really important things in your life.

Does it make sense to give up a weekend every April to figure out the latest changes in the income tax law so that you can prepare your annual income tax returns? Depending on the complexity of your tax situation, perhaps it would make more sense to delegate that task to an accountant, pay a fee, and free up the same time to do something more productive and meaningful to you. (Aren't I good at spending your money?)

■ **Hired help could** *be the solution you have been looking for – how about getting someone to look after the kids to take some of the pressure off you?*

STEP 10:
DECIDE WHAT AND TO WHOM YOU CAN DELEGATE

Take a look at all of your appointments and scheduled events coming up. Review all the discretionary items built into your to-do lists for as far ahead as you have them. Look at each and every item and ask yourself, "Is doing this task the best use of my time?" If it is, plan to do it. If it is not, try to figure out a way to delegate that item to free your time for the more important things.

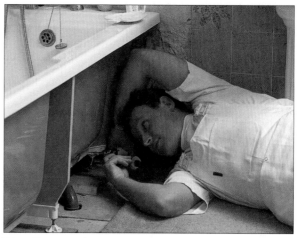

■ **Call on expert** *help if you are not sure how to do it yourself – it will save you time and effort.*

A simple summary

✓ Delegating tasks to staff members can leverage your time. If you need someone to help you, ask!

✓ Reverse delegation keeps your time free and preserves the relationship with that person who is trying to delegate their problem to you.

✓ Your inner circle of family, friends, and coworkers will probably be willing to help if you ask.

✓ Hiring a college "gopher" can get you 10 or 20 extra hours each week.

✓ Hiring some extra help might make more sense than trying to do it all yourself – and it will probably get done much quicker.

✓ Step 10 for organizing your life is to decide what and to whom you can delegate.

PART THREE

Chapter 11
Maximizing Meeting Time

Chapter 12
Using a Clean Work Area

Chapter 13
Managing Paperwork

Chapter 14
The Time Log

GETTING MORE ORGANIZED

Y OU'RE FINALLY GETTING organized! In Part Three you'll learn how to *maximize* meeting time and discover how a clean work area can give you a better *focus*. You'll

also learn how to more easily handle the daily paperwork that can overwhelm you and lower your productivity.

I'll share with you a simple yet powerful tool, the time log, that will help you take an *inventory* of how your time is actually being spent so that you can quickly make adjustments to better organize each and every day. Let your journey continue!

Chapter 11

Maximizing Meeting Time

A MEETING IS WHEN TWO or more people get together to exchange common information or to share information. What could be simpler? And yet, meetings are some of the biggest organizational time-wasters you will encounter at work. You need to be selective about the meetings you will attend and avoid the ones that are unnecessary. In this chapter I'll discuss how you can do just that.

In this chapter...

✓ Is this meeting necessary?

✓ Is your attendance necessary?

✓ Create an agenda

✓ Assign a time and stick to it

✓ Do away with amenities

✓ Step 11: Determine what future meetings you can skip

MEETINGS DON'T HAVE TO BE A WASTE OF TIME

Is this meeting necessary?

THE STARTING POINT *to effectively manage meetings is to ask yourself,*
"Is it necessary?" "What would happen if the meeting did not take place?"
"What would be the harm if we did not hold the meeting as often?" A lot of
the time we attend the meeting because we have always attended the meeting.
It may have become a habit that has outlived its usefulness.

In the United States alone each day there are some 17 million
meetings. It is a wonder that anything at all gets done at work!

In one-on-one
meeting situations,
ask yourself the
same question, "Is it
necessary?" Don't give
out meeting time to someone
just because the person asks for
it. Ascertain whether or not the
person really needs it.

■ **Don't feel obliged** *to agree to a*
meeting request simply because you
have the slot free.

What's on the agenda

A neat question I use to determine whether a meeting is necessary or not is, "What's on the
agenda?" For example, a legal client called me one afternoon and asked if I would be
available to meet with him 2 days later at 2 p.m. I checked my calendar and the slot was
available. I responded, "Yes, I am free then. When we meet, what's on the agenda? This way I
can better prepare for our meeting." He replied that he needed to know about some scheduling
issues relative to his file. "Is that what you need?" I asked. "Let me put you on hold, I'll
get your file, and I will get you the information you need now." In 5 minutes I got the client
what he needed in what would have taken the better part of an hour had we met in person.

Now I got paid by the hour for that work, but all of our time-management decisions
should not be made based on what produces the most revenue. Instead, we need to ask
ourselves, "What is the best use of my time?"

■ **Do you need to be in the meeting at all,** *or could your time be spent more effectively doing something else?*

Is your attendance necessary?

ASSUMING THE MEETING is necessary, ask yourself a second question, "is my attendance necessary?" What, if anything, would you get out of this meeting? As I've emphasized throughout this book, there are two ways to spend your time: wisely and not so wisely. We all have the same number of hours in a day, and it's up to you to use that time to your best advantage. A huge influence on how you spend your time comes from others. Many around you may have a better idea about how they feel you should be spending your time, and that may include attending many meetings.

■ **By using your time wisely** and making the right decisions you'll find you can spend longer doing the things you really want to do. Learn to judge how best to use your time.

Your time is precious

We have to take responsibility for designing our own lives. Of course, this doesn't mean we shouldn't listen to the counsel and advice of other people. It is useful that we do, but we must filter that advice in light of the ultimate direction in which we wish to go. When you have done your daily planning and know where you are going, there is no question in your mind how you should be spending the next day. It's when you don't have a clear vision of where you are going that you may feel the temptation to substitute working hard – and perhaps you feel attending as many meetings as you can means you're working hard.

Don't agree to give meeting time to someone just because he or she asks for it. Find out whether or not the meeting is really necessary. Is it the best use of your time? If it is, agree to the meeting. If it isn't, try to get out of it.

Am I required?

Ask yourself: Do I contribute anything to this meeting? If I don't attend, will anything be lost? Is my attending the equivalent of not attending? Do I get anything out of the meeting? Is my life enhanced in any way as a result of attending this meeting? Am I better armed with information to help increase my success?

If the answer to these questions is "no," see if you can get excused from the meeting, see if someone else can take your place who will be able to get more from it, or see if you may be excused from the meeting early, after what it relevant to you has been covered.

I served as a full-time college professor for some 15 years and during that time I was required to attend faculty meetings about every other month. I'm talking about over 200 people assembled in an auditorium, every one of whom makes their living standing in front of people and speaking. You can imagine how those meetings were! Everyone had a point of view and a desire to enter his or her two cents' worth. These meetings would drone on, often for hours, and after 15 years of attending nearly 100 of these faculty meetings, I can report to you that little was ever accomplished.

Trivia...

I speak to many people who use meetings as a way to substitute for their productivity with activity. Meetings in which many issues are discussed can be a way to look productive, but little action is actually taken. It is often difficult to follow up with these people to ask why they do this because they are – you guessed it – always in meetings.

Dealing with necessary evils

After attending a few of these meetings early on, it was easy to see that they were not necessary and it was not necessary for me to attend. I approached my boss, the department chair, to try and get out of this dreadful waste of time. I said, "These meetings are unnecessary and it is unnecessary for me to be there. Can I be excused?" My boss replied, "I agree. The meeting are a waste and it is not necessary for you to attend."

■ **Unfortunately there** *are meetings that you simply must attend – learn to grin and bear it!*

But then he reached into his desk and retrieved my personnel folder. He took out a copy of my faculty contract and continued, "But here in paragraph three of your contract it states that you shall attend faculty meetings. If I let you off the hook, I'd have to let everyone else off as well." "Wouldn't that be a tragedy," I thought.

Some things in life you can change. Some things in life you cannot change and you just have to live with. By making the request that you be excused from a meeting, you'll feel better that at least you've tried, even if you're turned down.

Since these meetings were going to be a necessary evil for me, I became very good at looking like I was involved in the meeting when I would really be doing something else, like correcting papers for my students or reading a book. Sometimes when we are forced to spend D time, of no value, we can convert it to A or B time, crucial or important. With good organization and control of your time, you don't have to allow outside circumstances to control your potential for success.

Create an agenda

JUST AS YOU PREPARE an agenda for your day during daily planning to focus the next 24 hours on the most important issues, it's important to have an agenda for your meeting. You, or whoever runs the meeting, may have a good idea about what is to be discussed, but what about the other participants? They need to know what topics will be addressed so they can prepare for the meeting.

Be prepared

Has this ever happened to you? You go to a meeting and the moderator turns to Mary and says, "Mary, tell us about the new health insurance program we are thinking about adopting." Mary is blindsided and totally unprepared to address this issue. She has no response or tries to dance around her lack of knowledge with useless information that wastes everyone's time. With advance notice, Mary might have indicated she would not be ready to discuss that topic at the meeting, so it could be removed from the agenda and save everyone time. Or perhaps Mary might have suggested that another item or two be added to the agenda that relates to this issue.

Don't have meetings by ambush. Let the participants know in advance what is to be discussed so everyone has an opportunity to be prepared before they come to the meeting.

■ **Don't go into** *a meeting feeling unprepared – there is nothing worse. Create an agenda in advance so that you and your coworkers are fully aware of what is going to be discussed.*

Assign a time and stick to it

HAVE YOU EVER *shown up on time for a meeting scheduled to begin at 2 p.m. and only three of the ten expected participants are present? And what do we do? Most of the time we wait and we wait until about 15 or 20 minutes after the hour when everyone eventually shows up, and then we start the meeting. When this occurs, we are punishing the people who obeyed the rules and were on time. This is not right.*

■ **If everyone involved** *prioritizes the meeting, it will start on time. It is also important to schedule time for each item on the agenda.*

■ **When you are part** *of a team you simply can't afford to let anyone down by being late.*

There are some out there who truly believe they cannot make meetings on time because of the unique responsibilities they have with their position. These people are always running late to the meeting, keeping others waiting because of what they have to contend with.

What's the hurry?

So here's how it happens. This person is in their office at 1:56 p.m. The meeting is at 2 p.m., and with all the good intentions in the world, she now proceeds to leave her office to go to the meeting a few doors down. As she is going out their office door the phone rings. She answers it. "This could be something important," she thinks. "And it will only take a minute." ("This will only take a minute" ought to be banned from our organizational vocabulary because it seldom "only takes a minute.")

Our friend completes her telephone call. It is now 2:04 p.m., but she has to make a quick phone call to Joe as a result of the phone call. This takes 3 minutes. It is now 2:07 p.m. and our friend is in the hallway on her way to the meeting, a bit late, and one of her team members, Doris, approaches with what appears to be the most urgent question ever. What does our friend do? She stops and listens to Doris. "I have to," she explains. "I can't turn my back on Doris. She's one of my key players. And after all, this will just take a minute."

It is now 2:21 p.m. and our friend has just arrived at the meeting 21 minutes late, having kept nine others waiting, which is a loss of over 3 hours of the organization's productive time. Our friend is convinced that she could not have been able to do otherwise. "You don't understand the responsibilities I have to deal with," she rationalizes.

Musn't be late!

But here is the irony. The same person who can never seem to make the meeting on time is never late for a 3:45 p.m. flight. Here is what happens in that scenario.

It is 1:56 p.m. Our friend, now in her office, has just 4 minutes to get downstairs to the front of the office building to catch the last bus to the airport to make her 3:45 flight on time. This is the last opportunity to get transportation to the airport. If she misses this bus, she will not make her flight.

She proceeds to the door and the phone rings. She lets it ring. She has to. She can't take the risk of getting bogged down in this phone call. The phone call goes wherever it goes to and would go to if it came in just a few minutes later when she was not there to hear the phone ring. Heading down the hallway, Doris, her key team member, approaches with an urgent question. What does our friend do? She says, "Doris, your question is very important to me. I will call you when I get to the airport so we can thoroughly discuss it."

Different situations, different priorities

So what's going on? Our friend is simply making different choices. If she can make choices that get her to the airport on time, why can't she make the same choices to get to the meeting on time? And the answer is, she can. I know there are exceptions to every rule. Emergencies do occur. What I am suggesting is that whether we make meetings on time or are habitually late probably has little to do with our external responsibilities and more to do with our internal rules and standards.

Can you see why it's so important to schedule time for each item on the agenda? For example, from 2 to 2:20 p.m., Joe will discuss the Smith account and from 2:20 to 3 p.m., Beth will discuss the new software package to be installed. You don't have to get locked into these time segments, but rather, use them as a guide to segment the time of the meeting for specific agenda items.

Without assigning time for each item, the first item on the agenda may take the entire meeting time because most people can go on forever about anything.

■ **Use the same criteria** *for getting to meetings on time that you use for getting to the airport in time for your flight.*

Too much talk

Some years ago, I was attending a PTA meeting at my son's elementary school. There were over 200 people in the auditorium. There were ten items on the agenda and the meeting was scheduled to last for 2 hours.

The first item on the agenda was, "Should the PTA advance $75 for the teacher supply fund?" A motion was made for this proposal, it was seconded, and then the floor was opened for discussion. The first person to the microphone spoke for about 5 minutes in favor of this proposal. She noted, "The teachers have been good to our kids. They need some additional supplies. We have the money from our dues and we should give them what they have asked for." This made perfect sense to me. I felt strongly that I would vote in favor of this proposal when it came up for a vote.

Then a second person offered her opinion at the microphone. "No," she said. "This is not what the PTA ought to do. This sets the wrong precedent. Our funds ought to be used for assemblies and special events. I think the Board of Education should fund this request. I am voting against this proposal." This got me thinking. Maybe I should not vote for this proposal. Maybe it would cause more harm than good. I was feeling unsure about which way I should go on this important issue. I felt that I needed additional input.

Well, I was in luck. There were now 12 other people standing in line before that microphone waiting for their chance to express their view and opinion of this important issue. It lasted an hour and a half. Some 300 man-hours to decide the issue of how we should spend $75. Halfway through this process, a father next to me elbowed my side and said, "Why don't we each kick in $37.50 and be done with this?"

■ **Put people in front of a microphone** *and they will go on forever, since it can give them a feeling of power and importance.*

Stick with the program

But don't you feel that way sometimes? Some things in meetings go far beyond what the value of the final outcome produces. That's why you should set aside a specific amount of time to discuss each item. If time runs out and the issue is still not resolved, plan to reopen the discussion at a future meeting.

After each item on the agenda is dealt with, schedule a follow-up. Decide what action needs to be taken and assign someone to make sure it gets done so that meetings are not a place where the same items are discussed over and over and the same solutions are offered once more – and still nothing happens.

Trivia...

Microphones are very dangerous things at public meetings. Most people don't have the opportunity to use them frequently, and there is such a feeling of power when we do!

■ **Make sure the agenda is followed,** *that notes are taken, responsibilities are assigned, and follow-up meetings are scheduled rather than going over the same issues in every meeting.*

Do away with amenities

IMAGING SHOWING UP to a meeting room where you always sat in nice plush leather chairs only to discover the chairs were removed? (People will not stand for that!) What would happen? Your meeting would probably be over a lot more quickly without the chairs than with them. The more comfortable you make a meeting, the longer it is likely to last. The less comfortable a meeting, the shorter it is likely to last. I am not for making things uncomfortable but it is a simple truth.

So, if you would like to have your meeting linger on, bring in the big comfortable leather chairs, turn up the heat to a cozy level, and be sure to serve refreshments. Your meeting will last a long time. If you care to shorten it up, however, don't add those amenities.

Avoid the comfort zone

Ever notice that the plastic molded seats found in most fast-food restaurants are designed to be just a little smaller than the average person's behind? The average person tends to get uncomfortable in this arrangement after several minutes. Why do fast-food restaurants do that? Because they don't want you to sit in their restaurant occupying the seat all day with a cup of coffee. Yet, if you visit a swank, plush restaurant, the seats are spacious, the lights are low, and the comfort level is enhanced because the owner wants you to stay.

Right place, right time

You can use this to your advantage. Let's say you have to meet with your insurance professional this Saturday. You need the information she will provide for you but you don't want to spend a lot of time with the person. Therefore you might suggest that you meet at a local fast-food restaurant. On the other hand, if you are to meet with someone about a career opportunity where the more time you have with that person, the more success you may have, you may choose a fancy, plush restaurant as your meeting place. The venue of the meeting place will often influence the length of the meeting.

■ **Comfortable and pleasant surroundings** *only encourage people to linger longer. If you want to have a short meeting, don't hold it in the best restaurant in town.*

Impromptu encounters

Finally, we sometimes have to deal with unannounced and unplanned meetings from drop-in visitors. I had a boss like that. He would come by unannounced, sit in my side chair, prop his feet up on my desk, and ramble on for an hour about almost nothing. I suppose if you allow that to continue you are teaching that person that the behavior is okay. We teach people how to treat us by the way in which we allow them to treat us. When I got rid of the side chair, the boss did not come by as often or for as long. Another technique to handle unwanted visitors is as to stand up, lean forward, and ask, "Yes?" as they approach. It creates a sense of urgency on your part that sends a message to most that maybe this is not the best time to interrupt you.

Some meetings are not designed to dispose of specific agenda items but are set to brainstorm. They are creative exercises to come up with solutions to various challenges and problems facing the participants. This type of meeting does not readily lend itself to the structure discussed in this chapter and are more free-flowing without the guidelines of times set for each item.

■ **Before you agree** *to have a meeting, make sure that your presence really is required – your time could be better spent elsewhere.*

STEP 11:
DETERMINE WHICH FUTURE MEETINGS YOU CAN SKIP

Look at your future appointments and scheduled events. Look closely at all meetings that are coming up. Review each and ask yourself whether the meeting is necessary and, if so, whether you need to attend. Do what you can to get out of attending those meetings that are unnecessary.

■ **Good organization** *starts with closely reviewing how you spend your time.*

A simple summary

✓ If a meeting is not necessary, determine whether or not it should be held in the first place.

✓ If your presence at a meeting is not required, try to get excused from attending.

✓ Create an agenda so that everyone has the opportunity to be prepared.

✓ Assign every item on the agenda a time and stick to it.

✓ People's sense of priorities are not the same, but that's no excuse for wasting colleagues' valuable time.

✓ Doing away with amenities like comfortable chairs and refreshments will naturally cause a meeting to end sooner.

✓ Step 11 for organizing your life is to determine which future meetings you can skip.

Chapter 12

Using a Clean Work Area

WHEN YOU HAVE TOO MUCH before you there is a tendency to become overwhelmed. You direct your attention to the tasks that can be accomplished quickly, which may not be the best use of your time. You can limit the choices you have before you, thereby getting a tighter focus, by working with a clean work area in both your work and personal life.

In this chapter...

✓ If it's out of sight, it's out of mind

✓ If it's in sight, it's in mind

✓ Our focus goes to the easy and fun stuff

✓ Clean it up!

✓ Step 12: Schedule a date to clean up your work area

A NEAT AND WELL-ORGANIZED WORK SPACE LOOKS GOOD – AND MAKES YOU FEEL A LOT BETTER, TOO

If it's out of sight, it's out of mind

I RECOMMEND THAT you consider working with a clean work area. If it's out of sight, it's out of mind – if you don't see it lying on your desk, you won't feel you have to address it right away, adding to your stress.

Is this you?

There are some people who work with a messy desk or work area. They may actually claim they do their best work in that environment! Do you know the kind of people I am talking about? They have stuff all over the place. Piles of paper on their desk, around their desk, on shelving next to their desk, and a bunch of stuff on a table behind their desk. (They have to go out and buy more furniture just to put this stuff on!)

And whenever you suggest to someone that he clean up his work area, does he get defensive! He says things like, "This is my external filing system" or "A cluttered desk is the sign of an organized mind." And if you really push hard he will almost always say, "But I know where everything is!"

■ **Unfortunately**
it's not always easy to make someone tidy their work area unless you are their superior, or they have a real desire to do so.

I know you can effectively multi-task and enhance your results. It is possible to be on the telephone and writing something at the same time. The problem is when you try to accomplish too many things all at the same time, you diffuse your efforts and reduce your productivity.

Focus your mind

Actually, how organized your work area is has a direct impact on your productivity. Here's an example. Let's say I go outside to the parking lot in the bright sunshine with 20 pads of notepaper and a magnifying glass. My task is to burn up all the pads at the same time using the magnifying glass to get a concentration of the sun's rays.

■ **An untidy work area** *leads to untidy work; by endeavoring to keep your paperwork in order and filed away you'll be more able to prioritize your tasks.*

I focus the bright sunlight through the glass onto the first pad and soon it begins to smolder and a flame appears. I rush now to the second pad. Why? Because I want to burn up all the pads at the same time. I focus the sun's rays through the magnifying glass on the second pad and soon it begins to smolder and a flame appears. But the flame on the first pad dies out. So I'm back to the first pad getting that lit again, and then to the second pad to re-ignite that one, and then off to the third pad because I want to burn them all up at the same time . . . you see how it goes.

After this frenetic day I probably still have 20 pads of notepaper in front of me with a lot of burned marks on each, but I still haven't burned up one complete pad of paper.

What if I only have one pad in front of me at a time? I can concentrate my efforts on burning up that one pad. It's the same with tasks. Having many to-do items before you creates a pressure to get them all done at the same time. If your work area is messy, with papers and projects strewn all over, you will feel that pressure more than if your area was organized.

If it's in sight, it's in mind

WE HAVE DONE STUDIES on this issue through our Productivity Institute and found that a person working with a messy desk or work area can, during the course of a full 8-hour day, waste as much as an hour and a half being distracted by all that is in front of him. Why? Because, if it's in sight, it's in mind, and we cannot help but be distracted by what is in front of us.

Now this is not a solid block of time but rather, a few minutes here and a few minutes there. "I know I should be working on that report, but let me handle a few of these phone messages first." "Here is some interesting junk mail." It's like a leaky hot water faucet, drip, drip, drip. Not a huge loss, a few drips at a time, but at the end of the day, gallons of hot water have gone down the drain.

If you waste 1½ hours per day, that's 7½ hours per week, or approximately 15 percent of the average workweek being diverted by a messy desk. Imagine being able to re-capture just half of that time and redirecting it to a more productive use.

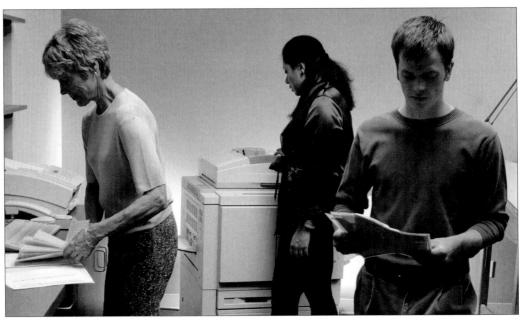

■ **Try to concentrate** *only on the task at hand; you may need to photocopy or fax a document, but wait until you've finished one thing before starting the next.*

Our focus goes to the easy and fun stuff

AS I MENTIONED in Chapter 8, human beings naturally seek out what is pleasurable and avoid what is painful, otherwise we tend not to act. So, when faced with crucial items, which are typically long and difficult to accomplish, and not-crucial items, which are typically quick and fun, we tend to do the not crucial items first, the pleasurable items.

Too much information

When I was in college, there was a student on my dormitory floor who loved business books. Almost every Saturday he would make the trip to the local bookstore and return with a new business book. He would show it to others on the floor and then put it in its proper place in the bookshelf above his desk where he had dozens of other business books he had purchased. He arranged these books alphabetically by title. It all looked so neat.

One Saturday, he took all the books from the shelving above his desk in his room and put them all on the floor to replace them back on the shelving, only this time, he grouped the books by subject matter. The management books were all together. The marketing books were all together. Over the 3 years we were together as students he took those books down and back again each time rearranging them with a different scheme.

In those 3 years he never read one of the books. Why? Too many choices. He was overwhelmed. Looking back, if he only had two or three books available to him at a time, he probably would have read them.

Don't give yourself too many choices. You can easily become overwhelmed by too many tasks and wind up accomplishing none of them.

■ **Arranging everything immaculately** *is completely pointless if you don't then use those resources.*

Clean it up!

I AM ASKED SOMETIMES how to get others to clean up their messy desk. Unless you have specific authority over that person where your order must be followed, we really can't get others to clean up their work area unless they have a desire to do it. You can lead a horse to water but you can't make him drink, as the old saying goes. But if you're the one working with a messy work area and have the desire to clean it up, the procedure is simple.

Pencil it in

First, set a date when you plan to clean up your messy work area. Make it the highest priority, an A-1 task in your to-do list for that day: "clean up messy desk work area." When the big day arrives that you have scheduled to clean up your work area, start by taking each piece of paper on your desk in hand and asking yourself, "When will I work on this item?" Perhaps this is a research project and you think you will be able to work on it next Tuesday. Then under next Tuesday's to-do list, add "Do research project" and then put that item away in a folder to be retrieved next Tuesday.

■ **Why not set** *a good example to the rest of your coworkers by letting them see the benefits of keeping their work areas clean and tidy.*

Smart filing

The next item is a company report. Again, ask yourself, "When will I work on this item?" Maybe you can tackle this next Wednesday. Under next Wednesday's to-do list, add "Do company report" and then put that item away in a folder to be retrieved next Wednesday.

Continue the same procedure with each item. If you have a lot of stuff on your desk this might take all day, but it's worth the effort. Spending the time now to organize your work area will pay off in increased productivity later.

■ **Sort all your paperwork** *into different categories or box files so that you can see at a glance what you need to tackle each day.*

Trash the trash

I had a student in my time-management seminar some years ago who made an interesting statement in our class. He had been a plant manager for 8 years, and he honestly did not know what the top of his desk was made of. He wasn't joking. He did not know if it was made of wood or metal because he had never seen it.
It was buried under paper several layers deep.

This plant manager picked up on my suggestion of working with a clean desk. In fact, he chose the first day after his seminar to begin work on this project. He made it his A-1 task for the day to clean up that messy desk one piece of paper at a time. It took him all day to do it. He found things in that pile that were 2 and 3 years old – old meeting agendas, coffee-stained memos, and correspondence he ought to have responded to a long time ago.

INTERNET

www.get-a-grip-on-your-life.com/

If you're feeling overwhelmed, check out this interesting site for tips and techniques to help you regain a sense of control over all areas of your life. It includes links to other helpful sites as well.

He set aside a pile of reading material – periodicals, magazines, and technical items he had accumulated over the years. The pile was over 2 feet high! "I threw it all out," he later told me. "The stuff was a D. It had no value. Some of the things in it were over 3 years old." "Why did you hang on to it?" I asked. "Because I never had a license to toss it out. Until I went through each thing on my desk, item by item, to determine its value, it always appeared to have value. This reading pile had no value, and once I figured that out I could throw it away, but until I did it owned me. Every day I would come to work and be reminded by the presence of that reading material of one more thing I was neglecting, adding to my stress. And it was all unnecessary."

Sense of order

Now, this plant manager works with one, two, or perhaps three items in front of him at a time. Every project has its own folder, so he can put all the paperwork associated with that project into the folder. This lessens the chance he will misplace anything. The projects he is working on that day go in a step file on his desk so he has easy access to them. Everything else is filed away but noted for action in a future to-do list so that item does not slip through the cracks and get overlooked. Even small changes make a difference. He now keeps all of his pens and pencils in one holder, his notepads in another, his floppy disks in another. His productivity has increased significantly just through the consistent practice of working with a clean and organized work environment. By following the same techniques, yours can too.

■ **It is amazing** *how quickly paper accumulates, so learn to throw unnecessary items away.*

Visit your local office supply store to check out all the neat gadgets and organizational tools that can help you organize your desk and work area. Cleaning up your work area can be fun!

A fresh start

This plant manager does one other thing that has made a big difference in his productivity: when he goes home at night he puts everything away. He leaves with a clean desk so that when he returns the next morning he comes in to a clean desk. There's a big psychological boost in arriving every day to a clean desk. Why is this so important? You and I are going to have some bad days filled with stress and frustration. We go home, recharge our batteries, and return to work the next day. The first thing we encounter is that mess we were working on the day before. And where does our state of mind go? To where it was yesterday, and yesterday was not such a great day, filled with stress and frustration. Taking a few moments at the end of each workday to put papers away and organize your desk means you can start fresh each day.

You probably start each day with clean clothes, a fresh new lunch in your lunch bag, and a new to-do list. Start each day with a clean desk by leaving with a clean desk the night before.

Sure, you may think, this all makes sense. You can follow these suggestions and clean up your work environment, but the very next day you will get more paperwork, deal with some of it, and set the rest aside. After a few days of getting additional paperwork, dealing with some of it, and setting the rest aside, you will once again be buried in a blizzard of paperwork.

So how do you keep from getting buried in a blizzard of paperwork? That is what we will address in Chapter 13.

■ **Start each day** *with a clean desk, in the same way you begin the day with fresh clothes.*

STEP 12:
SCHEDULE A DATE TO CLEAN UP YOUR WORK AREA

Decide when you will clean up your disorganized work area. Enter this task an action statement on your to-do list for that day.

■ **Schedule a date** *and time in your diary to clean up and organize your work area.*

A simple summary

✔ If it's out of sight, it's out of mind. We don't see it and we don't have to deal with it.

✔ If it's in sight, it's in mind, and you can't help but be distracted by those items which may not be the best use of your time.

✔ Focus goes to the easy and fun stuff because we seek pleasure and avoid pain.

✔ Too much clutter can interrupt your focus as you become overwhelmed by unnecessary information.

✔ Cleaning up your work area is as easy as setting a date to do it and then taking one item at a time and putting it away.

✔ Step 12 for organizing your life is to schedule a date to clean up your work area.

Chapter 13

Managing Paperwork

DOESN'T IT SEEM LIKE we are getting buried in a blizzard of paperwork in our jobs? The fax machine, interoffice memos, and even e-mail all contribute to this deluge. The problem is that instead of dealing with paperwork just once and then moving on, we accumulate it, review it, remind ourselves of what needs to be done, and then find ourselves repeating the same process with the same paper a day later. This increases the chance that we will miss deadlines and it lowers our productivity. You need to learn how to manage paperwork so that it doesn't manage you. I'll show you how in this chapter.

In this chapter...

✓ Getting off the lists

✓ Screening your paperwork

✓ Dealing with paperwork

✓ Managing e-mails

✓ Step 13: Getting a handle on your paperwork

YOU CAN AVOID A LOT OF HEADACHES IF YOU LEARN HOW TO MANAGE YOUR PAPERWORK

Getting off the lists

ONE OF THE BEST WAYS *to deal with a problem is never to have it in the first place. Look at all the* paper *you receive over the next couple of weeks, item by item, and identify the things coming to you that you do not need to receive. Analyze everything that comes at you and ask yourself what would be the result if you did not have this document before you. Has it provided you with useful information or not? Does it just occupy your time without any benefit?*

DEFINITION

For our purposes, **paper** *refers to any physical communication that you receive and that you can accumulate, including mail, memos, junk mail, faxes, e-mails, and voice mails.*

Rate each piece, using A for "crucial," B for "important," C for "of little value," and D for "of no value." Immediately make arrangements to stop the flow of the D items. Contact the sender and ask to be taken off the mailing list. You need not be offensive about it as you request your removal. You might say, "Joe, I want to save you a lot of time. You are sending me a lot of copies of your memos and they really are not of much value to me. Could you please remove my name from your list? It will save me time but, more importantly, it will save you time, because you won't have to keep sending me these copies."

■ **Voice mail and e-mail** *can be just as much of a burden on you as paper mail, so you must learn to control them in the same way.*

People will respond readily to your requests when you give them a reason to cooperate. People intuitively want to be of help especially when they have a reason to help.

Help others out

I always use the "ask-because" technique to get the cooperation of others.
There was an experiment conducted one time in an office. People were lined up at the photocopier machine waiting their turn to make their copies. Someone would come to the person in the front of the line several times during the day and ask simply, "Can I cut in front of you and make my copies now?" Twenty percent of the time, the person at the front of the line would agree and allow this new person to cut in line and make her copies first, but 80 percent of the time the person was told to go to the back of the line and wait for her turn like everyone else.

Later, this person would return to the copier line a few more times where a different group of people waited in line for their turn to make their copies. The person would go to the first person in line and ask, "Can I cut in front of you and make my copies now? My boss just gave this to me and he needs these copies immediately because he is leaving for the board meeting." Phrased this way, 80 percent of the time the person was permitted to cut in line and make copies, and only 20 percent of the time she was told to wait her turn like everyone else.

■ **People are more willing to** *help others if they are polite and have reasonable requests, so if you don't want to get stuck at the back of the line at work, or on the way to work, make sure you use the right phrase.*

What was the difference? In the second example, the person gave the first person in the line a "because," reason for her special request. It did not appear that she was just trying to create a special advantage for herself but, rather, that she had a valid reason to slip in ahead of others who had already paid the price of waiting in line. It says a lot to me about the goodness of human nature. People like to help others, especially when they are given a plausible reason.

Your name's on the list

Do you receive a lot of unwanted solicitation mail? It is sometimes referred to as "junk mail" because some of the recipients view it as junk, of no value. I don't want to unfairly criticize the mass mailing organizations who are trying to sell their products and services through unsolicited offers in the mail. I have responded to many of the offers and, indeed, I have used the technique myself as a marketing tool for our time management seminars. Many people enjoy receiving the catalogs and offers. It can be entertaining and informative. But if receiving this stuff is taking your time unnecessarily and has no value to you, contact each sender and ask that you be removed from the mailing list.

You can remove your name and address from a lot of mailing lists by contacting: Direct Marketing Association, 1120 Avenue of the Americas, New York, NY 10036-6700; phone (212) 768-7277; fax (212) 302-6714; Web site: www.the-dma.org.

■ **If you find** *you are being swamped by junk mail, take positive action – contact each company and ask to be taken off their mailing list.*

■ **You'll feel much more** *in control of your time if you receive only the mail you want to receive.*

Look hard at the C items, those that have little value. Look at each item and decide whether or not you want to continue to receive it. You might want to stop the flow of some but not all of these items, since a few of them may have some value.

You will want to continue to receive the A and B items because, by definition, they are crucial and important. These are the things that keep you in the loop and will have a benefit in one or more of your seven vital areas.

Don't feel obligated to continue receiving paperwork that you don't want. It is unfair to appear to others that you are welcoming their unwanted communications.

Screening your paperwork

IN CHAPTER 9 I told you about the importance of delegation as a tool to leverage your available time. The hardest part of delegation is frequently just letting go. We take great pride in doing things ourselves, but we only have so many hours each week to create our results so we need to be discriminating on how we spend our time, and that includes dealing with paperwork and electronic mail. A good question to ask yourself is, "Is this the best use of my time?" If it is, proceed with the task. If it is not, try to figure out a way to delegate to multiply your results.

Staff person

I have employed a staff person to screen my paper items first. She deals with the items that she is equipped to handle and then passes the rest on to me for my follow-up. Lots of routine things are then handled without my involvement. She prepares standard responses, does filing, tosses out things that have no value, and forwards items to others as necessary. I then receive only those items I need to deal with. It is a great time-saver.

■ **It can be hard** *to delegate and let someone else handle your correspondence, but it will save precious time.*

Many people don't have the luxury of having a staff assistant to help with their incoming paper items. Budgets and the real world may not permit it. But before you pass on this notion, if you know that having a staff person might help you to filter some of your paperwork and you don't have access to one, try thinking about ways to get one.

College and high school internships offer opportunities for assistance to people in both nonprofit and for-profit businesses. Our local high school has a program that places their business students out in the real world for 10 to 15 hours per week without cost. You need to provide training for these young people and provide them with real-world experiences. Why not consider having an intern join your organization for a couple of hours per day to help you out with processing and handling paperwork? You will manage your time more efficiently and the student will acquire life skills for the future. Everyone wins.

Group self-screening

Perhaps you don't have access to a staff person and the intern concept is not feasible where you are. Consider group self-screening, where you and your coworkers help each other by rotating as a screener for each other.

For example, let's say there are five of you who work closely together. On Monday, person #1 does the initial screening of the incoming paperwork for the entire group, including himself. He tosses out the junk and passes along the important information to each person in the group. On Tuesday, person #2 does it for the entire group, including herself. During one day a week, each of you will have the responsibility of screening for the group. Everyone saves time.

The best way to deal with paperwork is to handle it once. This frees you up to continue working on other tasks.

■ **If you can't** *afford to employ an assistant, why don't you and your colleagues take turns dealing with incoming mail, paperwork, and screening calls?*

Dealing with paperwork

SOME GO THROUGH *the pile of stuff on their desk in the morning reminding themselves of what has to be done and what has not been accomplished. Then they get caught up in other things during the day while the pile sits on their desk, crying for attention. The next day, these people are thumbing through the same papers as the day before, and with a few more additions, sort of spinning their wheels and not making much progress. Occasionally, deadlines slip through the cracks and opportunities are lost.*

■ **Piles of paperwork** *are counter-productive and may lead to inefficiency and further stress.*

I want you to get out of the shuffling blues and get the paper dispatched appropriately and efficiently. As you encounter paper, choose one of the following three options. You will handle your paper once and do what needs to be done more effectively and with less effort.

1.) If it's quick, do it right away

If the item will take only a minute or two to complete, do it right then and there. If you don't, by the time you complete the process of scheduling it and filing it away for future action, you could have done it. For example, if someone sends you an invitation to a staff meeting that requires an RSVP, take a moment or two to respond whether or not you will attend. Do it now and get it over with. In 10 minutes you can complete ten or more of these small items, getting them off your desk so that you can move on.

■ **Deal with easy items** *right away, instead of "filing" them for another day or putting them on your to-do list. This will give you the gratification of accomplishing more in less time.*

If it ain't broke, don't fix it. If you like receiving unsolicited mail offers, do nothing. But if don't care to receive them, do something about it.

2.) Delegate it

As you encounter each piece of paper, ask yourself, "Is this the best use of my time?" If it is, plan on doing it. If it is not, try to work out a way of delegating it to someone else (see Chapter 10 for specific ways to delegate tasks). After all, there is a lot of difference between "I do it" and "It gets done." Which is more important? It gets done!

■ **If it isn't necessary** *to deal with an item yourself, delegate it to your assistant or a colleague: the important thing is to get it done.*

3.) Schedule it

If the new paper item is going to take any appreciable amount of time, schedule it. Decide when you are going to have time to do it, put it on an upcoming to-do list for that day, and then file it away so that it's out of sight and out of mind.

Let me share a few ideas about filing systems. Over the years, I have tried any number of different ways to file things away for my future retrieval and use. I have used color-coded files with multicolored dots on the tabs for various categories. I have had them cross-referenced alphabetically by subject. I have filed and refiled.

When organizing your paperwork, don't choose a filing system that is so complex you will never use it. Simple is usually best.

Now I use a very simple alphabetical system for a personal filing system. I generally work with around 200 files for the projects, seminars, and clients and I work with. I file all of this alphabetically. The files are within a few steps of my desk. It sounds like a lot of files, but I pretty much know what is in each and I have immediate access, as I need a particular file. When the work is done in a file, I file it away in another simple filing system, my alphabetical archive file. Nothing fancy, but it works.

Managing e-mails

E-MAIL IS ELECTRONIC PAPER, *and ought to be treated the same as any other paperwork. It's interesting that as new technology is introduced, it is frequently heralded as the wave of the future that will save us all so much time, but often this works in reverse. There has not been much of a loss of first-class mail to e-mail. First-class mail is holding its own, but e-mails are soaring.*

■ **Computers were** *supposed to save us time, but e-mails have simply been added to paper correspondence, doubling the amount of mail we receive.*

Managing e-mails

If you receive a lot of jokes, chain letters, and other no-value e-mails, ask that your name be taken off the sender's distribution list. These kinds of e-mails can really add to the number of e-mails you get each day, and they take time away from other e-mails that are really important.

I get around 300 e-mails a day. That's a lot. A lot of them are junk and easily deleted. Many are for requests for free time-management articles that we send out to people who have requested them through our web site. Those requests can be handled by my assistant. But many of my e-mails require some time to read and a thoughtful response.

When I started using e-mail, it would take me most of the day to respond to it all. I would come to my office in the morning and download the overnight e-mails from my server. It would take a couple of hours to respond to all of them. I would click the Send button and off they would go around the globe. I would then click the Receive button and typically 20 or 30 new e-mails would be received. I would respond to these, click Send, and off they would go. I then would click Receive and get several more e-mails. As I continued this procedure, I found I could easily spend the bulk of my day at my computer, reading and responding to e-mails. In fact, it was as if I was a gambler addicted to the slot machines at the casino. "Just one more pull of the handle . . ." It never seems to have an end.

Some e-mail programs, like those available through Microsoft's MSN service, permit you to block the receipt of unwanted communications for addresses that you don't care to receive e-mail from.

■ **Sending and replying** *to e-mail can become addictive – the more you send the more you receive, and so on, until you are hooked!*

I have taken better control of my e-mail by applying the Rule of Three. I check my e-mail three times each day with three rotations of receiving. For example, I come into my office in the morning, download the previous night's e-mails, respond, hit the Send button, and off they go. Then I click the Receive button again to get a second batch of e-mails. I respond to this group, send them, and hit the Receive button for a third time. I respond to this last batch and then the computer is shut down.

About mid-day, I turn the computer on again. I access and respond to the morning's e-mails in this three-step process of receiving and responding. This process is repeated one more time at the end of the day so that I deal with e-mails three times each day. The e-mails are being handled effectively, but I am not forced to spend all day doing it.

■ **Joke e-mails from your friends** *can be very amusing and provide a break from the monotony of work, but just think of the time you are wasting reading and responding to these e-mails.*

It's in the in-basket

We use in-baskets in our office to manage the physical flow of paper. Each of us has one on our desks. If I need to deliver something to my secretary, I don't interrupt what she may doing at the moment. I put it in her inbox. She does the same for me. Then, a few times during the day, each of us will retrieve the paper that is in our in-baskets and take appropriate action on each item.

This is so much more effective than constantly interrupting one another throughout the day, because every time we get an interruption, we are thrown off track and have to take a few minutes to get back on track. Now, we don't want to throw common sense out the window. If there is an emergency, we will communicate immediately, but otherwise, it goes to the inbox.

INTERNET

www.getorganizednow. com

Take a look at this web site for hundreds of ideas on organizing your home, office, and life. You can also sign up to receivetheir free newsletter and get a free Get Organized Now! Idea-Pak filled with 50 tips on getting organized.

■ **Develop a system** *of passing work to your colleagues that avoids interrupting them.*

STEP 13:
GETTING A HANDLE ON YOUR PAPERWORK

Set aside a couple of hours to review all of the paper you have been receiving recently, including memos, faxes, junk mail, e-mails, and voice mail. Identify the C and D items that are of little or no value and commit to taking action to stop the flow of these unwanted communications.

■ **Perhaps you are** *spending too much time opening mail each day when your time could well be spent on other, more important, activities.*

A simple summary

✔ To reduce the amount of paperwork you get that's of little or no value, ask the senders to remove your name from their distribution list.

✔ Have your paperwork screened by a staff person or with self-screening so that you only have to deal with the important stuff.

✔ Deal with paperwork once by either handling it immediately, delegating it, or scheduling it in your to-do list for the items that will require more attention.

✔ E-mails are electronic paperwork and should be handled the same way as other paperwork.

✔ Save time by only downloading and replying to e-mails three or four times a day.

✔ Step 13 for organizing your life is to get a handle on your paperwork.

Chapter 14

The Time Log

NOW THAT YOU HAVE all these tools to better manage your time, it's important for you to clearly measure how your time is being spent so that you can more effectively apply the tools we have discussed so far. The device I like to use to accomplish this is a time log. By using a time log, you will get a clear picture of how and where you are spending your time.

In this chapter...
- ✓ It's like a photo album
- ✓ Using a time log
- ✓ Here's what you'll discover
- ✓ Step 14: Schedule your time log

IF YOU FEEL LIKE TIME IS RUNNING AWAY FROM YOU, KEEP TRACK OF IT IN A TIME LOG

It's like a photo album

*A **time log** is like a photo album. It permits us to take little snapshots from time to time and put them into an album so that we can see the big picture of how our time is being spent.*

DEFINITION

*A **time log** is a tool you can use to record how your time has been spent and how your that affects your productivity, so that you can take corrective steps to get better organized and to increase your productivity.*

A problem that is well defined is mostly solved. In order to better manage our time, we need to know where we are. We have to measure that progress in order to manage it. You may run the time log and discover that you are managing your time more productively that you thought. Most, however, find that there is a lot of room for improvement to better manage their time.

The time log frequently shows us how we typically spend more than we thought to accomplish a particular function. I'm not sure why, but when we try to estimate how long something will take to complete, we almost always underestimate it by 50 percent. For most of us, it typically takes twice as long to get something accomplished as what we planned. Most of us do not have a good and accurate clock in our heads to estimate how much time a task will take or how long a task took.

■ **Stop and consider** *how you spend your time. What steps could you be taking to get better organized and increase your personal productivity?*

Get started!

The time log is a simple tool to use. Start by breaking your day into the nine major ways you spend your time. In the sample provided on p. 223, this person spends time in meetings, on the telephone, selling, dealing with interruptions, reviewing the mail, doing research, reading, with personal/family matters, and miscellaneous. Some of these categories might be appropriate for you. If they're not, change them to fit your particular situation.

Make several copies of the blank time log on p. 222 so you'll always have a supply on hand.

Then put the date in the upper right of the time log and the starting time in the upper left corner. This person is starting their day at 8:25 a.m.

Then, periodically throughout the day, stop and log in how you spent the previous period of time. The first entry in this time log is at 9 a.m. How did this person spend the previous 35 minutes? Doing daily planning. Note how this is recorded in the far right column under Misc. The function is noted as planning and then in the small box, the function is rated as to its importance: A = crucial, B = important, C = of little value, and D = of no value.

■ **Once you start looking** *at how you use your time, you may be surprised by how long it takes to get from one meeting to the next.*

221

Using a time log

Time log   *General Categories*   Date:_____

Time of last entry		MIN		MIN		MIN		MIN		MIN		MIN		MIN		MIN		MIN	
	☐		☐		☐		☐		☐		☐		☐		☐		☐		
	☐		☐		☐		☐		☐		☐		☐		☐		☐		
	☐		☐		☐		☐		☐		☐		☐		☐		☐		
	☐		☐		☐		☐		☐		☐		☐		☐		☐		
	☐		☐		☐		☐		☐		☐		☐		☐		☐		
	☐		☐		☐		☐		☐		☐		☐		☐		☐		
	☐		☐		☐		☐		☐		☐		☐		☐		☐		
	☐		☐		☐		☐		☐		☐		☐		☐		☐		
	☐		☐		☐		☐		☐		☐		☐		☐		☐		
	☐		☐		☐		☐		☐		☐		☐		☐		☐		
	☐		☐		☐		☐		☐		☐		☐		☐		☐		
	☐		☐		☐		☐		☐		☐		☐		☐		☐		
	☐		☐		☐		☐		☐		☐		☐		☐		☐		
	☐		☐		☐		☐		☐		☐		☐		☐		☐		
	☐		☐		☐		☐		☐		☐		☐		☐		☐		
	☐		☐		☐		☐		☐		☐		☐		☐		☐		
	☐		☐		☐		☐		☐		☐		☐		☐		☐		
	☐		☐		☐		☐		☐		☐		☐		☐		☐		
	☐		☐		☐		☐		☐		☐		☐		☐		☐		
	☐		☐		☐		☐		☐		☐		☐		☐		☐		Total hours
Total time for day																				
% of day																				100%

Time log

8:25 *(start time)*   *General Categories*   *Date:* Monday, March 12, 2001

Time of last entry	Meetings	MIN	Telephone	MIN	Selling	MIN	Interrupt/ Daydream	MIN	Mail	MIN	Research	MIN	Reading	MIN	Personal/ family	MIN	Misc.	MIN
9:00																	A planning	35
9:12							D Bill	12										
10:00	C staff meeting	48																
10:10									B review	10								
11:15			B return calls	65														
12:15					A Smith	60												
1:15															C lunch	60		
1:35							D Bill	20										
2:45											A Jones quote	70						
3:15					B Jones	30												
4:00													B trade journal	45				
4:50	D sales manager	50																
5:10							C Bill	20										
5:30													B travel	20				
6:00													B newspaper	90			A planning	30
6:30															A dinner	30		
7:00																		
7:30															B news	30		
9:00													A self-aprov.					
11:00															C TV	120		
Total time for day	98		65		90		52		10		70		165		260		65	**Total hours** 875 min 14.6 hrs
% of day	11%		7%		10%		6%		1%		8%		19%		30%		8%	100%

The next entry is added at 9:12 a.m. How did this person spend the previous 12 minutes? Bill came by to complain about something. Note how that is entered under the column Interrupt/Daydream. Note its value was a D. Now, Bill himself is not a D. Bill is a great guy worthy of our love and respect, it is just that the time spent with Bill is a D, of no value.

The third entry is added at 10 a.m. How did this person spend the last 48 minutes? In a staff meeting. See how it is entered under the Meetings column. And note too how that block of time was rated, a C, of little value. Now what do you think that time would have been rated by this person's boss? Probably an A, crucial. But you don't want to put down what your boss thinks that time is worth. You put down what you think it's worth. Remember, it's your time we're talking about here. Continue writing in your time for the whole day.

■ **Office meetings may seem** *to be of the upmost importance to your colleagues, but rate them according to how useful they are to you.*

Be honest as you fill out the time log. No one but you needs to look at it. If you don't enter accurate information in the first place, you won't be able to take appropriate corrective action.

A useful tool

You may think it's a pain in the neck to run this time log and log in each block of time as soon as it's over. But it's important to do it as blocks of time are completed. Why? Because if you wait until the end of the day to fill it out, the time log will not be accurate. Remember, we don't have a particularly accurate clock in our heads to estimate how long something will take to accomplish or, looking back, how long something took to get done.

It's a good idea for you to run this log for several days to get a good idea of how your time is being spent. If you only run it for a couple of days, you may get a distorted sense of what is really going on in your days.

Here's what you'll discover

HAVING RUN YOUR TIME LOG *for several days, you will have accumulated some useful information. First, you'll discover how much time you are actually spending in each of the major areas of your day. In the time log sample, this person is spending 98 minutes in meetings, 90 minutes selling, 52 minutes dealing with interruptions from Bill, and so on.*

Then, along the bottom row, you can calculate the percentage of each day is devoted to the major function. In our sample, our friend is spending 11 percent in meetings, 10 percent selling, and so on.

■ **If you have filled in** *your log correctly, at the end of the day you'll be able to see just how much time you waste with distractions and how much real work you actually get done.*

Most people are surprised by the results they find from running their time logs. They think they have been spending their time in a certain way, but often they find they have been spending their time in a lot of other, more unproductive ways.

Making it all add up

Remember the Pareto Principle, or the 20/80 rule, as it's sometimes called, that I told you about in Chapter 4? The rule states that 80 percent of business comes from 20 percent of the customers. In other words, the small chunk of input produces the big chunk of output.

■ **You may be surprised** *to learn how you really spend the hours in your day – you may not have realized that all those coffee breaks do add up!*

Here is something else you can do with the data you accumulate from your time log. Get a plain sheet of paper and create four columns, A, B, C, and D. Now go back through the little boxes in each entry made in the time log and record the amount of time actually spent in each area under the appropriate column.

A	B	C	D
35	10	48	12
60	65	60	20
70	30	20	50
30	90	120	
30	30		
225 mins	270 mins	248 mins	82 mins
3.75 hours	4.5 hours	4.2 hours	1 hour 22 mins

The first entry was for 35 minutes of planning time, which was A time. Record 35 under the A column on this new sheet of paper. The next entry recorded 12 minutes with Bill and that was D time. Record 12 under the D column. The next entry was a C for the 48 minutes spent in the staff meeting. Record 48 under the C column. That's all there is to it. Continue for the rest of the blocks.

Now add up all the A time, the B time, the C time, and the D time to see where you've been spending most of your time. The result is likely to surprise you!

■ **Taking time to relax** *and recharge your batteries once in a while won't do you any harm at all – it will refresh and revitalize you making you better able to cope with a hectic schedule.*

Taking corrective steps

Do you think that in order to have had a good and productive day or week, 100 percent of your time ought to be in the A column? Probably not. I hope not, because that would be an unrealistic pressure on any of us. Are you going to have some C and D time in your day and week? Of course you are. You are going to look for it, aren't you? I do. I like C and D time. Not a lot of it, of course, but I find it's a good break from the focus on A and B items.

Don't worry about spending C and D time in your days and weeks. Good time management does not require that you are a machine working on A and B items only. C and D items deliver a welcome relief in our day and should be enjoyed in moderation.

Good week or bad?

Well, how about this as a result? If the majority of your time was spent on the A and B side and the minority of your time was spent on the C and D side of the ledger, would you feel like you had a good and productive day or week? I should think so. Did you have some wasted time? Of course. But it was the small amount of your day and week.

Now what should the numbers come out to? What would satisfy you? If 80 percent of your time was spent of the A and B side and 20 percent of your time was spent on the C and D side, would you feel you had a productive week? Well, how about 70 percent on the A and B side and 30 percent on the C and D side? How about 50/50? How about 20 percent of your time on the A and B side and 80 percent of your time on the C and D side?

Trivia...

To me, the most successful person is the person who decides on where they want to be and then achieves it. Don't you agree?

Here is the answer: You get to pick. There are no wrong answers. Any ratio is fine as long as that is your goal. How can I tell you that you are not a success unless you achieve a certain ratio between your A's and B's and C's and D's? I can't. I have no right to do that. That's the exciting thing about personal productivity. It's personal. So you establish the benchmark, the goal: 80/20, 50/50, 20/80, or anything else that makes sense to you and your life.

Achieving your goal

Whatever your target, the time log and the final analysis with the separate sheet of paper and the four columns for A, B, C, and D will show you how you are actually spending your time. If your analysis measures up to your goal, leave it alone. But if you have fallen short, being your numbers to a more acceptable level using the time-management tools and techniques in this book.

■ **With any luck** *the amount of time you spend on priorities will match your goals – at least most of the time – in which case you can continue to take that relaxing coffee break every day.*

If you would like something to compare your situation to, consider this. According to studies done by the Productivity Institute, the average person who conducts his own time log reports that, on average, only about 20 percent of his time is spent on the A's and B's, the things that are crucial and important, and that 80 percent of his time is being spent on the C's and D's, the things that have little or no value.

Working smarter, not harder

I was attending a Chamber of Commerce function a while ago and met up with a self-employed individual who operated his own printing service. He was one frustrated person. He told me how he was putting in over 70 hours per week, that he was not getting it all done, and how stressed he was. He always seemed to be dealing with interruptions that threw him off the track. Meetings? He said he wasted a lot of time in meetings almost every day. Delegation? He had a staff of six people and really could not delegate to anyone because they were "idiots" (that was his characterization, not mine).

■ **For some of us,** *work gets to the point where we don't think there's time to stop and organize the day – instead we keep swimming against the tide, trying to achieve the impossible.*

He was so frustrated that he was considering selling his business at a loss. Now there's a potential loss of productivity. He had to spend a lot of his time to accumulate the money to buy this business in the first place and now he was about to throw some of that past productivity away because of his frustration.

In my time-management seminars, I teach my students how to double their personal productivity, which seems like an elusive goal to many who feel they are working hard enough already. Many people equate doubling personal productivity to doubling the time or effort it takes to achieve results. They only seem to understand working harder rather than working smarter.

Less can be more

When he asked what I did in life, I told him that I teach time-management seminars that show people how to double their productivity. "Really?" he asked. "Do you think you can help me?" "Sure," I replied. "Oh, I get it," he continued. "If I attend your seminar you will tell me to go back and work 70 hours per week." "No," I said. "If you attend one of our time management seminars, I will tell you to go back and work only 35 hours per week." "I can't get it all done in 70 hours a week!" he cried. "You're going to cut my work week in half and then double my productivity? You don't understand your math functions. I need to work more hours, not fewer!"

"Let me explain what I think can be done," I replied.

We then talked about how the average person spends their time, spending 20 percent of their time on the A's and B's and 80 percent of their time on the C's and D's. And I had every reason to believe my friend was average. I don't mean this as a putdown, but all the things he was complaining about were the same things most of my time management students wanted to correct.

INTERNET

www.getmoredone.com

Create your own instant time profile by completing a questionnaire on a Time Tabulator designed by a consultancy, and compare the results to those of others in a similar position. Pace Productivity conducted surveys among employees and entrepreneurs in North America. Some of the results revealed how time is used in the average lifetime (e.g., 19 years working, 23 years sleeping), and how a workweek is split into tasks (e.g., 1.3 hours strategizing, 5.1 hours dealing with paperwork). While you're at it, take a look at the top time-wasters to target.

How do you spend your time?

I suggested to him, "If you are putting in 70 hours per week but only 20 percent of that time is A and B time, for things that are crucial and important, 20 percent of 70 hours is 14 hours per week of productive time, and the other 56 hours are spent on C and D items, things that have little or no value. These are things that ought to have been delegated, meetings that you should not attend, and interruptions you should not have to endure. I can share with you some simple but powerful techniques where you can change that ratio of time spent from 20 percent for A and B stuff to 80 percent for A and B stuff. Even if you were only putting in 35 hours in your work week, if 80 percent of those hours are A and B hours, 80 percent of 70 hours is 28 productive hours. With 28 productive hours out of 35 total hours instead of 14 productive hours out 70 hours, you can probably count on doubling your personal productivity in half the time."

He did not come to our time-management seminar. He did not have time. He was so busy doing it the wrong way, he could not take out a little time to learn how to do it the right way.

Use your time well

Here's another way to look at it. A woodsman works each day in the forest chopping wood with his ax. He cuts up two cords of wood each day for his customers. It takes him eight hours to do this. As time goes by, the ax gets dull and the only other variable he has to deal with is time, so he puts in more time to accomplish the same result to make up for the dull ax blade. What used to take 8 hours now takes 9. Soon it is 10, then 11 and then 12 hours to get the same output from this ax that gets duller and duller. The woodsman continues to work harder and harder to achieve the same result.

Then our woodsman gets a visit from someone from town who asks, "Woodsman, why don't you take a few days off and go into to town to sharpen up your ax?" Woodsman replies, "I can't take three days off for that. I'll be behind six cords of wood and my customers will be complaining!"

He will continue to work harder and harder to achieve the same results.

There is another woodsman out in the forest who is also working 12 hours to cut two cords of wood with his dull ax, but he has a different view of taking time off to sharpen up his ax. He makes the commitment to take a few days off to return to town to get his ax sharpened up. Sure, he too falls behind 6 cords of wood and his customers complain. But when he returns to the woods with his sharpened ax, what used to take 12 hours now takes 7. As a result of his investment in town, he can now accomplish his daily goal in less time.

■ **You'd take the time** *to sharpen or repair your tools if they weren't doing the job, wouldn't you? The same principle applies to the office: take time out to evaluate what you could be doing to increase your productivity.*

Even better, when he is in town sharpening up his ax, he learns about a new technology called a chain saw! Then when he returns to the woods, he can cut up four cords of wood with his new chain saw in an 8-hour day, literally doubling his productivity with the same time investment.

Running your time log will have a positive effect on your productivity as you will be able to see if you are spending too much time on non-essential tasks. Don't regard it as waste of your time — look at it as a way of reducing the amount of time you waste.

■ **If you take the time** *to reorganize your workday you will have the satisfaction of attaining your goals in less time.*

STEP 14:
SCHEDULE YOUR TIME LOG

Set a date to begin and run your time log for several days. Analyze your results and take corrective steps to eliminate the time-wasters in your life.

INTERNET

www.business.com

This web site offers lots of information on how to better manage your time, including links to sites such as managing finances, managing a home business, and sales.

■ **Your time is precious –** *don't waste it on trivial tasks.*

A simple summary

✔ A time log is like a photo album of your day so that you can view the big picture.

✔ To use a time log, just log in your data throughout the day.

✔ By using a time log, you can see how your time is really being

spent and what you need to fix to become more organized and productive.

✔ Don't be surprised if you waste more time than you think you do.

✔ Step 14 for organizing your life is to schedule your time log.

PART FOUR

Chapter 15
Dealing with Interruptions

Chapter 16
The Interruptions Log

Chapter 17
The Life Improvement Chart

Chapter 18
The 7 x 7 Technique

Chapter 19
*The Personal
Productivity System*

Chapter 20
*Practices for Your
Personal Life*

LIFE'S A BEACH, SO ENJOY IT!

MORE TIMELY TOOLS

I N PART FOUR I'LL outline more timely tools to add the finishing touches to better organizing your life. Here you'll learn how to control all of those *interruptions* that may keep you from doing what you need to get done in your day. I'll show you how a simple tool called the life improvement chart can help you identify where you really want to go in each of your seven vital areas. It will become a lifetime *roadmap* for your success.

You'll learn about the 7 x 7 technique that gives you added pleasure and success in your life with only a 10-minute investment of your time each day, and about the personal productivity system, a permanent *guide* to help you to keep all the important tools together for organizing your life.

Chapter 15

Dealing with Interruptions

WOULDN'T IT BE DELIGHTFUL if you could plan your day the night before, list all the things you have to do and all the things you want to do, prioritize that list, and then know for sure that would be how your next day would unfold? It seldom works that way. As the saying goes, life is sort of what happens to you along the way when you have planned something else. You will almost always experience interruptions throughout your day that will throw you off track. In this chapter I'll show you how to deal with interruptions effectively.

In this chapter...

✓ Life's little unanticipated events

✓ Good and bad interruptions

✓ Step 15: Keep a log of who you interrupt

NOT ALL INTERRUPTIONS ARE A BAD THING, BUT TOO MANY CAN BE DISTRACTING

Life's little unanticipated events

YOU DON'T KNOW WHEN *they will occur or how much time they will take. You can't plan them into your schedule. You just know that you will have* **interruptions** *from time to time during your day that keep you from doing all the tasks on the to-do list you made the night before. Interruptions usually come from others, but they can also come from you. As you proceed through your day, you may think of additional things to work on that you may have overlooked the previous night in your daily planning.*

> **DEFINITION**
>
> *An* **interruption** *is an unanticipated event; for example, phone calls, people dropping by unannounced, an unexpected shift in job priorities, or the call of a beeper.*

Interruptions find their way to us either in person or electronically. An example of an in-person interruption is when you're at your desk and a coworker stops by to ask about a project you are working on, or you are home and a neighbor drops in to chat. Electronic interruptions come to you via the telephone, beepers, e-mails, or pagers.

■ **Interruptions are a reality** *of the modern world: phone calls, beepers, and e-mails all compete for our attention.*

Good and bad interruptions

EVERY INTERRUPTION CARRIES with it some sense of urgency. To the interrupter – the person giving you the interruption – it is almost always something crucial in need of immediate attention. But to you – the person receiving the interruption – the priority is often a lot lower.

Grading the interruptions

There are good and bad interruptions. A "good" interruption has a value of A (crucial) or B (important) to you. A lot of what you do on a day-to-day basis is to handle the A and B interruptions. A customer calls with a new order, your child needs attention, or a coworker drops by with questions that only you can answer – these are all what most would consider crucial and important interruptions.

Then there are the C (of little value) and D (of no value) interruptions, those that are of little or no value to you. Perhaps a coworker drops by your office to chat about her weekend, or you get a phone call from a telemarketer who wants to sell you a magazine subscription. These "bad" interruptions may cause you concern because the time you spend taking care of them keeps you from dealing with more important A and B matters, therefore lowering your productivity to some degree.

There may be times when you like getting C and D interruptions. We don't have to be productive all the time, and everyone needs a break once in a while. The point is, you choose when. You maintain control.

■ **Some interruptions are** *more valuable than others. Interrupting your work to take care of a sick child is one of them.*

The ones you get paid to handle

How do you handle the various interruptions that come your way in an average day? First, let me describe how a lot of people handle interruptions. Most people turn their attention first to the most current and immediate request. For them, the squeaky wheel gets the grease; the loudest voice gets their attention. They respond in proportion to the person's sense of urgency in delivering the interruption. Why? Because we have been trained to respond that way. We want to please, to serve, to say "yes." It is how we succeed in life.

The people-pleaser

Let's say it's mid-morning and you're working on an A-4 task from your to-do list, a project for work. Along comes Joe, one of your coworkers, with an interruption. It seems he needs some information that you have in your files about customer Smith. He asks that you get it for him immediately, because in his mind, this is crucial. It is a request that will take you the better part of an hour to fulfill. If you're like most people, you will set aside your current effort, the A-4 item, to accommodate Joe's request. After all, you want to be known as a people-pleaser.

■ **Don't fall into the trap** *of giving the "squeaky wheel" all of your attention. Try to focus on what your real priorities are.*

Steering you off-course

As you turn your attention to this new matter, perhaps another interruption comes your way. Your phone rings; it's a call from another coworker with information about a staff dinner that is coming up shortly. You then direct your attention to this newest interruption because it is the most recent voice calling for your attention, setting aside both the first interruption from Joe and your originally planned A-4 task. Maybe a few more interruptions come your way throughout the day. By the end of the day you have done a little work on many things, not getting much of anything done, not the least of which was your A-4 task, which you planned to do when you made up your to-do list the night before. You have been much like a leaf blowing in the wind, floating here and there based on the strength of wind gusts that came your way. You go home feeling a bit stressed and frustrated. Now there is nothing wrong with this approach of responding to interruptions as they come your way, and it will produce some level of productivity during your day. Of course, there are some interruptions that you'll need to handle immediately. If your boss comes to you and asks for some sales figures because he has a conference call in a half-hour, that's an interruption you need to deal with immediately. That is what you get paid to do. But there is a better and more productive way to deal with other more flexible interruptions.

Four steps to managing interruptions

You can't always control the interruptions that come your way, but you can often control the way you choose to respond to them. When you receive an interruption, instead of postponing the task you are currently working on and redirecting your attention to that interruption based on the urgency created by the person giving you the interruption, maintain control of the interruptions by doing the four things outlined below.

1 Get complete information about the nature and specifics of the request being presented to you. Be sure you have a clear idea of the nature of the task you must perform.

2 Ask the person giving you the interruption a very important question: "When do you need it?" Often we ask the wrong question, which is, "When do you want it?" Of course, the typical answer to "When do you want it?" is "Now!" and sometimes, "Yesterday!" This is because the person interrupting you probably considers the interruption crucial. He or she feels a sense of urgency and pressure to get what is needed right now. But when he may want it and when he needs it are often two different answers. The answer to the question, "When do you want it?" is almost always sooner than the answer to the question, "When do you need it?"

■ **A day of interruptions** is unproductive and can often leave you feeling tired, stressed, and frustrated.

Ask "When do you need it?" more than once to determine the absolute latest date when the person truly needs what he or she is asking you for.

243

■ **In order to** *accomplish a job to the best of your ability, factor in a realistic amount of time in which to do it, and don't shy away from bartering for more time.*

Let's say Joe comes to you and asks, "Can you get me the information about customer Smith's orders?" You reply, "You mean all the back orders that have been placed?" "Yes," Joe replies. You have taken the first step and gotten complete information about what has to be done. Then you should ask, "When do you need it?" Joe replies, "I need it this afternoon by 5 p.m.." This is his first response. You want to see if there is some flexibility. Many of us get caught in crisis management when a deadline approaches because we did not budget enough time to get a task done in the first place. We may be overly optimistic about how quickly we can accomplish things. Most often, things do take a lot longer to accomplish than we may have originally planned.

So, you will want to ask about the needed deadline a second time: "Joe, with all that I've already committed to do today, if I can't get this done for you by 5 p.m., would it be okay if I got it you by Wednesday of next week, 6 days from now?" Joe considers that for a moment and replies, "No, Wednesday will not work for me. I am going to need the final information for a meeting I have on Tuesday afternoon with this customer." "Okay," you answer. "Well, if I got this information to you by Monday afternoon by 4 p.m., would that be okay?" "Yes," says Joe. "Monday by 4 p.m. will be fine." You have now made a commitment to a later deadline than originally requested which is consistent with what Joe really needs rather than what he stated he wants. You have given yourself more time to get this task done.

Always allocate your time with as much control as the situation allows. Don't just comply with demands from others on your time.

3 Take advantage of the power of the pen. If you are interrupted with a request to do something, add the new task to your to-do list. Following our example about customer Smith, you might write at the bottom of your list, "Smith customer information for Joe."

4 Prioritize this new item. You are currently working on your A-4 task, the project for work. Ask yourself which one is more important: the A-4 task or this new item that came to you as an interruption? You can't work on the A-4 task and handle Joe's request for the Smith customer information at the same time. Trying to work on two tasks at the same time inevitably creates a bottleneck and leaves us feeling immobilized. The key is to prioritize competing demands.

■ **If interruptions are** *an inevitable part of your day, implement a system to manage them.*

Let's say you are standing in the middle of a bridge and are very hungry. To your left there is a banquet of fresh fruits and vegetables. To your right there is a banquet of ham, turkey, and roast beef, all yours for the taking. You may say to yourself, "I think I would like some of those sliced carrots to the left," and start moving toward them. But then maybe you think, "Well, it would be nice to have some ham first," and reverse course and start moving to the right toward the cold cuts. "Wait a minute – that broccoli sure looks delicious," and you shift direction again toward the vegetables.

As you continue this back-and-forth thinking, shifting the focus from one objective to the other, you waste time, get nothing to eat, and remain hungry. It's the same thing when you try to do two or more things at the same time. To be productive, you need to prioritize all those demands that are competing for your attention.

Since the new item, the interruption, is not due for several days, you might conclude that your A-4 item that you are currently working on is more important than the new interruption. Go to the next item on your prioritized to-do list, your A-5 item, and ask yourself is the new item, the Smith customer information, more important than your current A-5? Continue the process until you get a sense of where the interruption fits into your to-do list.

Prioritizing importance

Since the new interruption item is more important than your existing B-2 item, label the new interruption item, the Smith customer information, as B-2a and the existing B-2 item as B-2b. What do you do with any paperwork for the new Smith customer information item? File it away and direct your attention to your original A-4 item, the item you were working on before the interruption came your way. Continue with the items on your to-do list and you will get to the new interruption item you have added in order of its importance.

On the other hand, what if you feel the new interruption item, the Smith customer information, is the most important use of your time at the moment because Joe really does need it immediately? Then the new item will be labeled as an A-4a and your existing A-4 becomes A-4b. Now, direct your attention to the new interruption item, the A-4a. When it is done, your attention returns to the A-4b, the work project that you were working on before you received the interruption from Joe.

■ **Some interruptions** *are our own doing – taking an extra-long coffee break, chatting with co-workers, or making personal calls, for example.*

What if you get a lot of interruptions during the day? Some business and professional people can get 50 to 60 interruptions in a single workday. You may be in a position to receive more or fewer than that, but whatever the number of interruptions you receive, you need a system to maintain control. Otherwise, you may get bogged down the entire day responding to the loudest voices.

Spending your day responding to interruptions without regard to their overall priority can be a productive way to spend a day. It just may not be the most productive way to spend your day.

The little things

Do you have to go through this four-step process for every interruption you receive? For example, someone stops by your work area and asks, "What time is it?" Do you reply, "Specifically, which time zone were you referring to? When do you need to know this?" and then add the request to your to-do list? Of course not! You will probably receive many quick interruptions in a day. These take just a minute or two to respond to, and you can deal with them then and there. Get them out of the way and then return to your to-do list.

■ **Prioritizing interruptions** – *taking care of the most important ones first - gives you a greater sense of efficiency and control.*

The ones that come from you

Interruptions don't always have to come from others. You can create them yourself. For example, let's say it's mid-morning, you are working on your A-4 task, and you happen to think of a new item that you should have added to your to-do list the night before. You can treat that like an interruption you might receive from someone else. Develop a clear picture in your mind of what has to be done. Decide when you need to get it done and add it to your to-do list. Finally, prioritize it in the mix of all the other items on your to-do list.

The ones you don't get paid to handle

Some interruptions may not be worth your efforts to respond to. These may include many of the C (of little value) and D (of no value) interruptions. If you're going to be effective about organizing your life and maximizing your productivity, it's important that you don't allocate your time based on those people who simply demand it. Why? Because the demands outweigh the supply of time available to you. You don't have enough hours in the day to satisfy all of the daily demands on your time. If you are going to increase your effectiveness, it's important to allocate your time on the basis of those who deserve it.

This doesn't mean that you should be uncooperative or rude to those around you. It is not arrogantly saying to others, "You are too unimportant and do not deserve my time." Rather, it takes into account that you have limits on your time, just 168 hours each week that can only be spent once, so be cautious and discriminating about how you spend it.

Just say "no"!

One of the most powerful words in your time management vocabulary should be "no." Saying "no" does not always require saying the exact word "no." Perhaps some of these might work when "no" ought to be the answer: "I'm sorry, I have so much on my plate now, I can't give this matter my attention"; "I don't when I'll able to help you on this, but I know someone over here who can help you now"; "I can't get it to you right away, but I will be able to do that for you before the end of next week."

> ### Trivia...
> *When the spring fever bug bites you, one of two things can happen. You can give in to it, blow off the day, move all of the tasks on your to-do list to another day, and feel guilty about it. Or you can give in to it, blow off the day, move all of the tasks on your to-do list to another day, and feel great about it. We all deserve a break once in a while to stop and smell the roses!*

You use the words you are comfortable with during each situation. My point is, if you are always in a position where you can never say "no," then you are always saying "yes," and while you may perform productively that way, you may not be as productive for the same amount of time spent. Do what you must to keep from getting bogged down in the C and D interruptions that keep you from doing the A and B things that enhance your productivity.

Every interruption costs you time just by occurring. If it takes you a minute to understand what the interruption is about and another minute to resume what you were doing, even a minor interruption has cost you 2 minutes. If you are getting dozens of interruptions in your day, those minutes can quickly add up.

■ **Succumbing to spring fever** *isn't a bad thing; taking a day off may help you wind down.*

"We interrupt this busy day . . . "

One other big interruption may come your way as you try to take action on your to-do list. Let's say you create a wonderful to-do list filled with all the things you have to do and want to do the next day. You can't wait to tackle those tasks for a super-productive day.

The next day is one of those first warm spring days after an unusually long and cold winter. The temperature is in the 70s as you start the day. You smell the scent of flowers and hear the music of the birds in the air. You then get bitten by the spring fever bug. It happens to us all. You are most likely going to blow off the day. Enjoy it! You are not some machine that functions without rest. The spring fever bug happens for a reason. It permits us to slow down, enjoy life, and recharge our mental batteries.

If you take a spring fever goof-off day early in March, will that affect your overall productivity for the year? Unlikely. Most of the things we need to do on a day-to-day basis can be pushed over to another day. Now, if you have made a commitment to someone to get something done today and they are relying on you, then you have to pay the price and get it done. I don't think many would disagree with that notion. If you have made commitments, you must follow them through. But for most of the daily things, a goof-off day of spring fever does us more good than harm.

■ **Taking time off** *to enjoy life usually has a positive impact on your job.*

STEP 15:
KEEP A LOG OF WHO YOU INTERRUPT

Keep a log of whenever you interrupt another person for a week or two. You may have a very long list. After gathering this data, go through each entry and decide which of the interruptions you brought to another were of the A (crucial) or B (important) variety and which were of the C (of little value) or D (of no value) variety. Take actions to avoid bringing C and D interruptions to others.

■ **If you keep a log** *of who you interrupt – and how often you interrupt them – you may be surprised by the results.*

A simple summary

✓ Life's little unanticipated events are inevitable and will keep you from completing the tasks on your to-do list satisfactorily.

✓ There are "good" and "bad" interruptions. For maximum productivity, learn how to handle and prioritize the good interruptions and avoid the bad interruptions.

✓ Learn to differentiate between the interruptions you are paid to handle and those you are not.

✓ Develop a system for dealing with interruptions so you avoid unneccesary distraction.

✓ Step 15 for organizing your life is to keep a log of who you interrupt.

Chapter 16

The Interruptions Log

YOU NOW KNOW THAT BOTH "good" and "bad" interruptions are an inevitable part of almost any day, no matter how well you plan for them. If you can get a clear understanding of your interruptions problem, you are most of the way toward finding a solution. To help you get a clear picture of your interruptions so that you can start to control them and reduce many of them, you need to prepare an interruptions log. I'll explain how to do that in this chapter.

In this chapter...

✓ Creating an interruptions log

✓ It's for your eyes only, so be candid

✓ What your interruptions log tells you

✓ Coworker interruptus

✓ Step 16: Keep an interruptions log

TO CONTROL AND REDUCE INTERRUPTIONS AT WORK, START LOGGING THEM

Creating an interruptions log

INTERRUPTIONS ARE A LOT like a leaky faucet. They drip and drip, seemingly not amounting to much, but by the end of your day, you may be flooded with gallons of water. The phrase in management science today is that if you want to manage it, you have to measure it. That is what an **interruptions log** does. It catalogs interruptions as they occur so that you can see the big picture of what is happening in your day.

Keeping track of your interruptions

Cataloguing your interruptions as they occur may seem like an inconvenient exercise, given all the other things you have to deal with in a day, but doing so does produce helpful information. You can use this information to take corrective actions to minimize those pesky C and D interruptions that take you away from doing the more important A and B tasks that enhance your productivity.

DEFINITION

An **interruptions log** *is a simple tool you can use to catalog interruptions as they occur so that you can take corrective actions to minimize them.*

■ **It may seem like** *a waste of time to catalog interruptions, but if you want to manage them you've got to measure them first.*

■ **Remember to keep** *a log of everything that keeps you from doing what you need to do. Information is power.*

Just get a pad of paper and write across the top, "interruptions log." Then create six columns and follow the instructions below:

1 *In the first column* record the date of the interruption.

2 *In the second column* record the time that the interruption occurred.

3 *In the third column* identify who or what interrupted you.

4 *In the fourth column* record a word or two to remind you what the interruption was about.

5 *In the fifth column* note the length of time in minutes that the interruption took.

6 *In the sixth column* place a value on the interruption: was it A (crucial), B (important), C (of little value) or D (of no value), from your point of view?

Simple, right? You might want to prepare one interruptions log for in-person interruptions (people dropping by) and one for electronic interruptions (faxes, e-mails, phone calls, and the like).

Run your interruptions log for 5 or more days to give you a fair sampling of the interruptions you incur. If you run it for a shorter period of time, you may get a distorted view of the problems. It's a good idea to run an interruptions log every few months to continue to maintain control over your interruptions.

When an interruption comes your way, note it on your interruptions log after you deal with it. Write down the date and time it occurred. Note who brought it to you, what it was about, and how long it took to resolve. Then be sure to give it a rating of A, B, C, or D.

■ **It's important** *to record and rate interruptions for at least 5 days to get the most out of your log.*

It's for your eyes only, so be candid

BE HONEST AS YOU *fill out your log, entry by entry, line by line. No one other than you has to look at this and see what rating you give to the interruptions you receive in your day. Typically, in the mind of the interrupter, the interruption is an A; otherwise, he or she probably would not have interrupted you in the first place. But don't put down what the interrupter feels it is worth. Put down what you feel it was worth. You are measuring how your time was spent. With the correct information input, you will be able to more readily identify and solve problems.*

To give you an idea of how this looks, here are two partial sample interruptions logs. The first is for in-person interruptions; the second for electronic interruptions.

INTERRUPTIONS LOG: PERSONNEL

Date	Time	Who	What	Length (min.)	Rating
6/1	9:02	Rick	Compare project notes	18	A
6/1	9:25	Bill	Complained about boss	12	D
6/1	1:40	Bill	Borrowed files	22	C
6/1	4:25	Amy	Asked about meeting	6	B
6/2	9:30	John	Chatted about weather	11	D
6/2	11:30	Susan	Help clear copier jam	10	C
6/2	2:10	Rick	Asked for Jones file	5	A
6/2	4:30	John	Borrowed book	3	D
6/3	9:00	John	Returned book	5	D
6/3	10:35	Susan	Help find copier toner	15	C
6/3	3:15	Amy	Asked for sales figures	20	A

INTERRUPTIONS LOG: ELECTRONIC

Date	Time	Who	What	Length (min.)	Rating
6/1	9:50	Fax	Order confirmation	3	A
6/1	10:35	E-mail	Meeting agenda	6	B
6/1	12:40	E-mail	Request for archived files	15	B
6/1	2:30	Phone call	Questions about project	22	A
6/1	3:12	Phone call	Telemarketer	6	D
6/2	8:45	Fax	Jones account info	5	A
6/2	10:00	Phone call	Confirm lunch w/client	10	B
6/2	2:35	E-mail	Questions on Wade acct.	15	B
6/2	4:00	Phone call	Follow-up on report	20	B
6/3	8:15	E-mail	Request for Miller files	18	A
6/3	1:30	Fax	Sales figures for last year	8	B
6/3	3:55	Phone call	Personal	10	D

Don't wait until the end of the day to fill out your interruptions log. It will be difficult to remember all the details, especially if you receive dozens of interruptions in your day. If you don't have accurate information about your interruptions to begin with, you can't take appropriate corrective steps.

Trivia...

The average business and professional person gets one interruption every 8 minutes. That's about six or seven interruptions per hour!

What your interruptions log tells you

WHILE IT'S CERTAINLY AN ANNOYANCE to have to add creating an interruptions log to your day-to-day responsibilities, it's a worthwhile task because it does produce a lot of valuable information. Having run your log for 5 or more days, what does the information that you've gathered tell you?

Planning around your interruptions

First, many people find that their interruptions occur within identifiable patterns. For example, I tend to get most of my interruptions early in the day and early in the week. The point is, if I then plan an important and time-consuming A-1 task for first thing Monday morning, I am typically buying stress and frustration.

Why? Because I no sooner get started on this large project Monday morning and the phone rings. It's a call from a client and I have to attend to it. After I get off the phone, a staff member comes into my office looking for some direction on a project he's working on. I can't turn my back on the request, otherwise his whole schedule could get bottlenecked. And on and on it goes, keeping me from getting much done on that important A-1 task that I scheduled into my to-do list the night before.

I've found it's a lot easier to swim downstream with the current than to try to buck the flow of the river. So knowing I get most of my interruptions early in the day and early in the week, I plan those larger, more time-consuming A-1 tasks for later in the day and later in the week when I'm likely to have fewer interruptions.

■ **Find out what** *your busiest times are for interruptions and plan to work around them.*

When are you busiest?

If you are working an 8-hour period, you probably get somewhere between 50 to 60 interruptions in a day. They are a big factor in most people's days. Now you may get a lot more or a lot fewer interruptions than the average person. Averages are, after all, made up of extremes. You run your own interruptions log to determine what is going on in your unique days.

The "date" and "time" columns on your completed log can help you identify if there are any patterns to when you receive your interruptions. If you see any patterns you can plan around them.

The "who" column can tell you a lot as well. In Chapter 4 I told you about the Pareto Principle, or the 20/80 rule as it is commonly called. To refresh your memory, the 20/80 rule states that typically, 20 percent of the input gives back 80 percent of the output. In other words, the small chunk of input is responsible for the big chunk of output. The other 80 percent of input will produce the other 20 percent of output.

■ **If you are constantly** *being disturbed when you are at your busiest, try to identify a pattern in the interruptions so that you can come up with a coping strategy.*

Interpreting information

Most people who share their completed interruptions log with me show that a relatively small number of the people they interact with (perhaps 20 percent, more or less) are responsible for the big chunk (perhaps 80 percent, more or less) of the interruptions they receive. The majority of the people they interact with (perhaps 80 percent, more or less) will be responsible for the small chunk (perhaps 20 percent, more or less) of the interruptions they receive.

When you review the "what" column you can see if the interruptions involved some common threads. Did the same person interrupt you with the same issue? Does one person have a habit of stopping by your desk every morning just to chat?

Record all interruptions, regardless of who did the interrupting. You are not criticizing the interrupter, but simply gathering information from which to take corrective steps.

Check the "length" column to see how much time you are spending on interruptions. The average interruption takes about 5 minutes. Some take a lot longer and some can be dealt within a short period of time. For example, your boss may come into your office unannounced at mid-morning and give you an assignment that will take the next several workdays to complete, throwing all of your plans out the window for the next few days. On the other hand, a coworker may come by your area and ask, "Can you show me where the toner is for the photo copier?" You comply in your usual helpful and cheerful manner and the entire task takes only a minute or two.

■ **How often do you plan** *for something to take an hour and it ends up taking twice as long? Interruptions are often at the root of the problem.*

A waste of time

If each interruption averages about 5 minutes to address, that totals to around 250 minutes in the day. When you divide that by 60 minutes, it comes out to about 4 hours per day of interruption time. That means that in an 8-hour day, you may be spending half your time dealing with interruptions!

The "rating" column is the most valuable. Percentage-wise, how many interruptions do you think most people find are A and B interruptions, things that are crucial and important, compared to C and D interruptions, things that have little or no value? After running an accurate interruptions log for 5 or more days, most people conclude that only about 20 percent of the interruptions they receive are of the A and B variety, interruptions that are worthy of their attention, and 80 percent of their interruptions are of the C or D variety, having little or no value to them.

If you are satisfied with your ratio of A and B interruptions to C and D interruptions, do nothing further. If you are not satisfied with your result, talk to the people who are interrupting you with matters of little or no value to you and ask for their cooperation in limiting their interruptions.

■ **If you want** *to be more efficient at what you do, calculate how much of your time is wasted on interruptions.*

Coworker interruptus

THE A AND B INTERRUPTIONS are worthy of the time you spent on them. A lot of what you get paid to do is to handle these types of interruptions. By definition they are crucial and important. It is the C and D interruptions that cause us concern.

Let's assume you are spending about half of your workday handling interruptions of all types. Let us further assume that 80 percent of them are C and D interruptions, of little or no value. That totals out to a bit more than 3 hours a day of wasted time getting caught up in interruptions that should not have occupied your time. What's the solution? Talk to the people who are bringing you the unimportant and unproductive interruptions and ask for their cooperation. Each case is different and requires a different approach. Most people will play by the rules once they are explained to them.

The diplomatic approach

Maybe one of your coworkers has a habit of dropping by every day to discuss personal issues. You might say to her, "I enjoy talking to you, but I need to get to work on this report. How about if we wait until after work when we'll really have time to talk about this? Or we could go to lunch today, if you're free." Perhaps another coworker comes to you frequently with the same type of problem, looking to you to solve it. You might want to plan some time with that person to teach him or her how to solve the problem themselves.

■ **If a coworker is** *constantly interrupting you, getting together to talk about it is an effective means of figuring out how to manage the problem.*

A problem solved?

Should you ever put a sign on your door asking that you not be interrupted if you're working on a critical project? Perhaps this one: "I shoot every third interrupter and the second one just left." Just kidding. Actually, putting a sign on your door may not be a practical solution. It may work once in a while, but if you use this tactic often enough, people will start to violate it. A better policy might be for coworkers to agree that every morning from 10 to 11:30 p.m. is "no-interruption" time, and during this time interruptions are not allowed.

Seeing a "Do Not Disturb" sign on someone's closed door can be construed as rude and antisocial (it's also impossible if you don't have an office door).

Another solution that might work for your office is to use in-boxes to cut down on the number of interruptions. For example, if you need some files from a coworker, rather than going to that person and asking for them, you would put your request into her in-box. Two or three times a day she would retrieve the items in her in-box and deal with them. This way items don't slip through the cracks and are attended to. Of course, if the building is on fire you want to know about it, but short of things of that urgency, most items can wait.

Two points of caution:

1. You will never be able to eliminate all the C and D interruptions. This is neither practical nor desirable. There may be situations where you don't feel comfortable confronting someone about bringing these lower-level interruptions to you, so don't do it. We aren't going for perfection here. If you can reduce your number of C and D interruptions by one-third, you will have regained 1 hour per day, 5 hours per week, and 250 hours over the next year – that's about 6 working weeks to focus your attention on things that are a more productive use of your time.

2. Idle chat about sports or whatever is not necessarily C and D time, even if you don't have an interest in the topic. There is a lot to be said for relationship building in the workplace, isn't there? Just the idea that someone, perhaps your boss, thinks enough about you that he or she may want to share an interest with you has a value. To you, that time might be a B or even an A. Assess its value in the context of all the considerations you may have.

I have found that a lot of C and D interruptions, when allowed, will mature into A and B payoffs later on. Be open to that possibility.

■ **A personal conversation** *with one of your coworkers shouldn't automatically be construed as an interruption; assess the value of all interruptions in context.*

It's all down to you

Here's a final thought. If you find you have a repetitive interrupter in your midst who brings you C and D interruptions on a regular basis, wasting a lot of your time, it's easy to blame that person and feel you are being taken advantage of. But I really believe most people treat you the way you allow them to treat you. That is, by allowing someone's behavior toward you, you are training that person to some degree to behave in that way. Take responsibility for your life. What happens, happens. That is not important. It is what you do about it that counts.

If a coworker is coming by each day asking for the same information, it's easy to blame that person for their actions. A more productive attitude is, "What is it that I am doing that is allowing this behavior to persist?" Haven't you been teaching the person that he can come to you for that information and you will provide it? Most of us take the easy way out and follow the path of least resistance unless we are challenged to do something differently. Until you stop letting that person take advantage of you and encourage him to seek out the information he needs himself, you should not feel like a victim.

■ **Take a look** *at your own behavior: Could you be encouraging people to interrupt you?*

STEP 16:
KEEP AN INTERRUPTIONS LOG

Commit to running your own interruptions log for 3 to 5 days. Then analyze your results and find ways to reduce some of the C and D interruptions in your day, giving you more time to handle more of the A and B tasks on your to-do list. It's a good idea to run an interruptions log every few months so you can assess your interruptions and take corrective steps on an on-going basis.

■ **Your interruptions log** *enables you to identify problem areas at work so that you can become more productive over the long run.*

A simple summary

✔ To begin to take control over interruptions, create an interruptions log. All you need is a pen and sheet of paper.

✔ Be candid as you fill out your interruptions log. No one else will see your log, and without accurate input, you can't take appropriate corrective action.

✔ Study the information on your log to see how you can reduce a lot of the unnecessary and low-priority interruptions that keep you from doing the crucial and important tasks in your day.

✔ The best way to minimize C and D interruptions is to ask people who are interrupting you to limit their interruptions.

✔ Step 16 for organizing your life is to keep an interruptions log.

Chapter 17

The Life Improvement Chart

I BELIEVE IF YOU ARE going to manage it, you must first measure it. Your biggest management job is the management of your life. The life improvement chart is a simple tool for you to measure where you are now and where you would like to be, and gives you the steps to get there. In this chapter I'll show you how to use the life improvement chart to improve the seven vital areas of your life.

In this chapter...

✓ How's your life going?

✓ Filling in your life improvement chart

✓ Prepare your chart twice a year

✓ Step 17: Schedule your life improvement chart

IT'S TIME TO TAKE POSITIVE STEPS TOWARD IMPROVING YOUR LIFE

How's your life going?

EVERYONE'S GOALS AND VALUES *change over time. A* **life improvement chart** *is a simple tool that can help you evaluate where you are and where you are going, whatever point you are in your life. As you determine how satisfied you are in each of the seven vital areas of your life (see Chapter 2) and compare it with where you want to go, you create a road map of what to do next in life. Without this direction, the tendency is to work harder rather than take specific action to move toward your goals, which may not yield the results you seek.*

DEFINITION

A **life improvement chart** *is a simple tool you can use to evaluate the quality of your life now and what it will take to significantly improve it. By using the life improvement chart you can take a quantum leap forward in improving the success and quality of your life.*

Take a look at the blank life improvement chart opposite. Notice it has four sections:

Rating Now Here is where you can take stock of your current situation and quantify where you are in your life.

Desired Improvements In this section you list those changes that you feel will make your life better – those things that will bring you a higher level of personal satisfaction.

Anticipated Ratings with Improvements Once the desired improvements have been implemented, what will the level of quality be like in your life, in a quantifiable, measurable way? Here is where you write it down.

Action Statements to Bring About Desired Improvements This section is where you list the specific steps necessary to achieve the desired improvements. These steps are then entered into your daily to-do list on the day you think you will start to take action on them.

Putting your goals and desires into writing brings them more within your control, making it easier to achieve them. You may have so many goals and desires in your head that they seem overwhelming at times – to the point where you don't have the motivation to get going on what you really want in life. That's where the life improvement chart can help.

LIFE IMPROVEMENT CHART

	RATING NOW			DESIRED IMPROVEMENTS	ANTICIPATED RATING WITH IMPROVEMENTS		
	RELATIVE VALUE	1–10 SCALE	TOTAL VALUE		RELATIVE VALUE	1–10 SCALE	TOTAL VALUE
Health	_____	x _____	= _____		_____	x _____	= _____
Family	_____	x _____	= _____		_____	x _____	= _____
Financial	_____	x _____	= _____		_____	x _____	= _____
Intellectual	_____	x _____	= _____		_____	x _____	= _____
Social	_____	x _____	= _____		_____	x _____	= _____
Professional	_____	x _____	= _____		_____	x _____	= _____
Spiritual	_____	x _____	= _____		_____	x _____	= _____

Total Quality Points _____   Total Quality Points _____

ACTION STATEMENTS TO BRING ABOUT DESIRED IMPROVEMENTS

Health

Family

Financial

Intellectual

Social

Professional

Spiritual

Filling in your life improvement chart

REFER NOW TO THE *completed life improvement chart opposite. Look at the upper left-hand section, "Rating Now." The first column is "Relative Value." Here you want to assign a value to each of the seven vital areas. On a scale of 1 ("very little importance") to 10 ("of utmost importance"), decide how important each of these seven areas are to you. As you rate your performance on the life improvement chart, bear in mind that each value is independent of the other. You can rate them all 1's, all 10's, or anything in between.*

■ **Ensure you know** *exactly what it is you want from life and don't be afraid to aim high.*

LIFE IMPROVEMENT CHART

	RATING NOW			DESIRED IMPROVEMENTS	ANTICIPATED RATING WITH IMPROVEMENTS		
	RELATIVE VALUE	1-10 SCALE	TOTAL VALUE		RELATIVE VALUE	1-10 SCALE	TOTAL VALUE
Health	10	x 6	= 60	Reduce weight to 160 pounds. Exercise daily	10	x 10	= 100
Family	10	x 6	= 60	More quality time Family activities ___ times a week	10	x 10	= 100
Financial	10	x 5	= 50	Increase income 30%	10	x 10	= 100
Intellectual	6	x 4	= 24	Read 12 books	6	x 10	= 60
Social	8	x 6	= 48	Social activities ___ times a week	8	x 10	= 80
Professional	8	x 5	= 40	Get promotion	8	x 10	= 80
Spiritual	9	x 8	= 72	Regular church attendance	9	x 10	= 90

Total Quality Points 354

Total Quality Points 610

ACTION STATEMENTS TO BRING ABOUT DESIRED IMPROVEMENTS

Health Start weight control by *October 3* Start daily exercise by *October 3*

Family Schedule family activities *3* times per week

Financial Develop additional income plan by *October 31*

Intellectual Read one book per month, *10* pages per day, starting *this weekend*

Social Schedule social activities *3* times per week

Professional Discuss promotion requirements with boss on *October 10*

Spiritual Schedule church attendance starting *this Sunday*

Assessing what's important to you

In our sample life improvement chart, this person has determined that his health, family, and financial areas are all 10s, of equal and utmost importance. His intellectual area is worth a 6 which means that, compared to the three above, it is only 60 percent as important. His social and professional areas are each valued at 8, which makes them more valuable than the intellectual area, but not as important as the top three. Finally, the spiritual area gets a 9. It has more value to this person than his intellectual, professional, and social areas, but is not quite as important as his health, family, and financial areas.

When you fill out your life improvement chart, don't feel you have to compare yourself to the ratings in the sample life improvement chart. Any rating you choose is fine. There are no right or wrong answers.

Next, refer to the middle column, the "1–10 Scale." This will record your actual performance, your current report card. It answers the question, "How are you doing?" in each of the seven vital areas.

Given that an area holds a certain level of importance in your life, how are you doing in that area? Again rate each area on a scale of 1 to 10. A 1 indicates the lowest level of successful, current performance in an area, while a 10 indicates perfection in that area, it just does not get any better.

■ **A Life Improvement Chart** *yields different results for everyone, depending on what you value most.*

■ **If a spiritual life** *is important to you, make time for it.*

Using the life improvement chart

In our example, this person is saying that his health area, while it is worth a 10 to him as a dimension in his life, his performance is only a 6, or he is only operating at a 60 percent level of potential performance. He feels there is a lot of room for improvement in that area. The intellectual area commands a 6 for its value, but his performance is at a 4. Again, there's a lot of room for improvement. The spiritual area is worth a 9 and his performance is an 8. He feels comfortable with how he's done in this area; there's not a lot of room for improvement.

Make several copies of the blank life improvement chart so you always have a supply of charts to work on.

Having completed both columns, we now multiply the two numbers in each row for each area and record the result in the third column labeled "Total Value." Referring again to the sample life improvement chart, health, which is worth a 10 and has a performance value of 6, the result then is 60 in the "Total Value" column. For family, which has an importance of 10 and a performance of 5, the result is 50. In our sample, when the "Total Value" column is added up it totals 354 Total Quality Points, which will become a meaningful number when we complete the rest of the chart and measure the Total Quality Points with Improvements.

The next steps

Now go to the "Desired Improvements" section of the chart. The objective here is to answer the question, "What would it take to make my 1–10 Scale just about perfect in each of my seven vital areas?" I know perfection is not an attainable goal, but look at it as more of a target to shoot for in your life. So, what would have to change in your life to make each area a 10 in terms of your actual performance?

In our example, this person is saying with respect to his health area, "If I can reduce my weight to 160 pounds and exercise daily, I feel my health will be a 10." In the financial area, "If I can increase my income by 30 percent, I will be satisfied that this area is a 10." In the professional area, "If I can get that promotion, this area will become a 10." You might require a lot more space to properly fill in this section than has been provided, as there may be a lot of new things to add in each area of your life to achieve greater happiness.

■ **Find out what kinds** *of changes you need to make in your life to achieve specific goals.*

Take action now

Refer now to the section of the sample life improvement chart, "Anticipated Rating with Improvements." The same Relative Values appear in the first column as were recorded on the left-hand side. Each still holds its same relative level of importance. What will change is the middle column, the "1–10 Scale." Here, all areas will score a perfect 10 for performance (again, an ideal). Once again we multiply the two numbers in each row for each area and record the result in the third column labeled "Total Value." Now, at the health row, this person winds up with 100 points of total value. You can't get any better than that. At the intellectual row, the sum is 60.

The "Total Value" column is then totaled. This person arrives at 610 "Total Quality Points" versus 344 from the "Rating Now" section to the left, before the desired improvements are factored in. In a measurable, quantifiable way, this person virtually doubles the quality of his or her life.

It is not enough to have a vision and a desire for change in your life to make it come true. You must take action different from what you have done in the past, because if you continue to do what you have always done, you will always achieve the same results (or non-results).

■ **Wishing and dreaming isn't enough.**
If you want to change your life you need to take action now.

■ **If your goal is** *to start attending church regularly, why not begin this Sunday?*

Set yourself targets

The final section, "Action Statements to Bring About Desired Improvements," is where you list the specific steps you need to take to bring about the improvements you seek, along with the deadlines for commencing action. If you don't include a deadline, you are likely to procrastinate. Did you ever make New Year's resolutions that you failed to follow through on? Sure, we all have! Without a deadline, it's easy to get caught up in other matters, and before you know it, weeks have passed and you still haven't taken any action.

In the sample, our friend will "Start weight control by October 3." He will "Develop additional income plan by October 31" and "Schedule church attendance starting this Sunday." These action steps are now included on a to-do list for the specific days for taking action on these new items.

Here is the chief value of preparing your life improvement chart. When you have developed a clear picture of where you truly want to go in this life in each of your seven vital areas and then work your way backwards to determine what you have to do each day, each month, and each year to get there, the choices you make on how to spend your time, day in and day out, is no contest. There is no question in your mind what you should be doing with your time tomorrow, this weekend, and next month when you are working toward specific goals. But if you don't know where you truly want to go in this life, the tendency is to work harder.

Hard work without any planning may not yield the results you seek. Working smarter will.

Using the life improvement chart almost automatically makes you better at organizing your life and managing your time. When you have a lifelong destination in mind you are excited about not only what you have to do each day, but by what you want to do each day. You may waste less time in meetings, tend not to get sidetracked by interruptions as often, and know when to delegate more often.

Schedule it

We never seem to get enough time to do everything we need and want to do in our lives. You have to take the time. Decide when you will start using your life improvement chart and make it an action item on your to-do list for that day.

■ **If there's something** *you really want to do — see good friends, for example — schedule a date!*

Prepare your chart twice a year

IT'S USEFUL FOR YOU to prepare and revise your life improvement chart twice a year. Why? Because your goals may change as you grow older and as different events occur in your life. Preparing your chart at least twice a year gives you a sharp focus of how you ought to be spending your time on a daily basis to achieve the things you consider important in your life.

Don't throw away your old life improvement charts. It's useful to go back through the ones you prepared in the past to see how you have changed and progressed. It shows a sort of continuing story of your life.

■ **Don't forget that** *as your life changes, your goals change, too. Take the time to revise your life improvement chart a couple times a year.*

STEP 17:
SCHEDULE YOUR LIFE IMPROVEMENT CHART

Set a date to sit down to work on your life improvement chart. Begin the process of leveraging the control you have over your future.

■ **Every moment** *of the future is precious – your life improvement chart helps you enjoy each of them to the fullest!*

A simple summary

✔ Quantifying where you are in your life and comparing that with where you would like to be helps motivate you to make improvements in your life.

✔ The life improvement chart is a useful tool for evaluating the seven vital areas of your life and how you can improve your satisfaction in each.

✔ Your vision for the future should be based on what you have done (or not done) in the past.

✔ Prepare your chart twice a year so that you create a continuing story of your life.

✔ Step 17 for organizing your life is to schedule your life improvement chart.

Chapter 18

The 7 x 7 Technique

ALOT OF GOOD COMES to us when we take little steps on a consistent basis and enjoy their cumulative effect over time. The 7 x 7 technique permits you to build in a series of little improvements in your day, beyond all the other organizing steps you have taken, to make each day a little more fun, a little more satisfying – and a little more productive.

In this chapter...

✓ A few little improvements each day can add up to a lot

✓ Making tomorrow a little better

✓ Acknowledging others

✓ What goes around comes around

✓ Step 18: List your seven little improvements for tomorrow

TAKE THE TIME TO ACKNOWLEDGE SOMEONE CLOSE TO YOU

A few improvements each day can add up to a lot

CAN YOU IMAGINE experiencing around 2,500 little improvements in your life over the next 12 months, taking no more than 10 minutes a day? Wouldn't your life be better with 2,500 little improvements? Sure! It goes without saying. Using what I call the **7 x 7 technique**, you can help make it happen. Practicing the 7 x 7 technique will not dramatically change tomorrow for you, but it will make the day a little sweeter and more fun.

DEFINITION

The **7 x 7 technique** is when you build one little improvement in each of your seven vital areas, 7 days a week, to get the equivalent of around 2,500 little improvements in your life over the next 12 months.

■ **Making just a few** *small changes every day can have a surprisingly positive effect on your lifestyle.*

Making a better tomorrow

EACH NIGHT AS YOU write up your to-do list for the following day, in addition to putting down all the things you have to do and all the things you want to do, and the specific action steps to realize your dreams and goals, take a moment to build in one little improvement in each of your seven vital areas. These are little improvements that you would not ordinarily think too much about and that don't take effort.

A little step at a time

Perhaps when you go to work you always try to park close to the front entrance. Tomorrow, make it a point to park on the other side of the parking lot and walk a bit further for a little extra exercise. Or maybe you take the elevator to the third floor. Tomorrow, walk up the stairs rather than ride the elevator. Maybe you've been meaning to lose a few pounds and narrow your waistline a bit. Tomorrow, skip the dessert that you usually enjoy after dinner, or eat some fruit instead. Now record this new task that you are going to accomplish on your to-do list for tomorrow under the health area. Put an asterisk (*) to its left to denote it as a "quickie" item that can be done in less than a minute; e.g., "* skip dessert."

■ **Modest steps** *can help you achieve your goals: if you have health concerns, opt for a better diet.*

Make a note of it

Under family, how about leaving a little love note under your partner's pillow or bringing home a surprise rose? My son used to take his lunch to school, and while he was brushing his teeth I would write a quick note: "Roses are red, Violets are blue. You're terrific, but so am I too! Love, Dad" and stick it in his lunch bag under his peanut butter and jelly sandwich. Then at lunchtime, he would shake the contents out of his bag and the note would fall out. Sure, he might have felt a little embarrassed getting a note from Dad in front of his friends, but the point is, he knew I was thinking of him and loved him. (And besides, when he arrived home that night, he had great fun "getting even" with me!)

■ **Often the smallest things** *mean the most. Exchanging photos and letters with faraway friends and family brings you closer together.*

It's in the mail

My in-laws don't get to see their grandchildren as often as they would like. We take a lot of pictures in our family, so when I get the processed photos back from the photo lab, I make it a point to send my dad and my in-laws a couple of snapshots. No letter – just label the pictures, put them in envelopes, and mail them. It only takes a few minutes. It gives me a good feeling all day and I know that they will get a kick out of receiving the photos. I put that little task down on my to-do list for the next day and put an asterisk to the left of this quickie item to remind me to do it, e.g., "*send photos."

Is it necessary to come up with something new in each area every day? Yes, if you want to get the full 2,500 improvements. But if you find a particular improvement works for you and you want to repeat it, great! Maybe you only get 1,000 different improvements in a year – that's fine too. Perfection is not the goal; making every day a little better is.

Imagine how delightful it is to get an unexpected piece of good news in the mail. You can extend the same joy to a loved one just by taking a moment to share something with that special person now.

■ **If someone close** *to you has done something special, or achieved something wonderful, show them how proud you are of them!*

TAKE STEPS TO IMPROVE YOUR LIFE

What little improvements could you make in your life in each of your seven vital areas? Here are some ideas to help get you started:

Health:
- Walk after dinner
- Take the stairs instead of the elevator
- No red meat for today

Family:
- Leave spouse a little note
- Send a card to Mom
- Volunteer to clean up after dinner

Financial:
- Set up an appointment with financial planner
- Get information on 401K plan at work
- Get new ATM card

Intellectual:
- Pick up new books at bookstore
- Read the newspaper cover to cover
- Call for adult education course catalog

Social:
- Set a lunch date with a friend
- Call friend just to say hello
- Give out a sincere compliment for a job well done

Professional:
- Set up time with boss to review company goals
- Check out business opportunity
- Use time log to track work time

Spiritual:
- Schedule church attendance
- Take a moment to count my blessings
- Schedule reading spiritual material

Put down one little improvement in each of your seven vital areas for the next day. You will have seven new entries, all "*" or quickie items. In less than 10 minutes you will achieve seven little improvements in your day tomorrow. Every day for the next week, build seven little improvements into your to-do list. At the end of the week, you will have accomplished 49 little improvements. Continue the process for the next year, and you will get about 2,500 little improvements in your life just by taking 10 minutes a day!

Don't try to remember all these improvements in your head. Write them down on your to-do list each day so you won't forget them.

Acknowledging others

I HAVE A STANDING 7 x 7 technique that I practice in my social area. Almost every day, I go out of my way to genuinely and sincerely compliment someone on something that I perceive to be of value that the person has done. Perhaps a coworker does a great job presenting sales figures at a meeting, or my friend receives a long-overdue promotion, or my wife prepares a wonderful dinner. Sometimes we get so caught up in our day-to-day routine that we forget to simply acknowledge those around us for their good work. A few minutes spent doing this can mean a lot, both to you and to the person you're complimenting.

■ **Make your loved ones** *feel appreciated when they do something nice for you.*

A lesson for life

Here's a story I'd like to share with you. We hold our monthly public time management seminar at a local hotel. One of the wait-staff is a fellow named Orlando, a delightful young man with a "can-do" personality. About an hour before our seminar was to begin one day, I arrived to find the seminar room in shambles. (The hotel does do a good job for us, but occasionally we all drop the ball.) I went into the corridor behind the function room and found Orlando. I explained the problem, how we needed to have the room set up before people arrived to make the seminar run smoothly. Orlando informed me that he was not assigned to our room, but nonetheless, he would take care of the problem. He went out of his way to make it right, getting the tables set with the right number of chairs. He could just as easily have told me, "I'm sorry, it's not my problem," but he didn't. The seminar began on time and ran smoothly, and I made a mental note to see Orlando before the end of the day and thank him for what he did.

■ **Don't forget to acknowledge** *the people who go out of their way to help you.*

At the end of the day, I found Orlando in the corridor and called him over. (The hotel manager was nearby, but I would have done this anyway.) At first Orlando was astonished, thinking, "What did I do wrong?" I said to him, "Remember the problem with the room this morning?" "Yes, was everything all right?" he asked. "It was perfect!" I told him. "You really went out of your way to get it straightened out, and I know you didn't have to do it because you had other rooms to take care of. I just wanted you to know how much I appreciate it, going out of your way the way you did."

Do you think Orlando appreciated those words? Sure he did. And, do you know, every month thereafter, when we are at that hotel, Orlando is always there making that little extra effort to make our stay more pleasant. (And that's not the end of my contact with Orlando, as you'll see in the next section.)

> Some of the most important words in the English language are "I love you," "Great job," and "Thank you." Everyone appreciates that occasional pat on the back or loving gesture. We never hear enough good words from others about all the good things we do.

■ **There's a lot of truth** *to the old adage, "What goes around comes around." If you send out a lot of love you're bound to get some back.*

What goes around comes around

WE'VE ALL HEARD THE SAYING *"What goes around comes around." Do you believe that? If you send out love in your life, what are you going to get back? Love. If you send out hate in your life, what are you going to get back? Hate. Maybe you know someone who complains that all he gets in life is hate and unhappiness. He typically blames the world for what he is getting. I would ask that person to take a hard look at what he's sending out. If you don't like what you're getting in life, take a look at what you are sending out. Do you want more love in your life? Send it out first.*

Let's say that over the next year you send out 365 compliments, deliver 365 surprise roses, and send out 365 surprise acknowledgment notes or greeting cards. First of all, it will be enough of a reward just to do it and see the reactions you will receive. But beyond that, do you think it's fair to assume that during the course of the year you might get back some of those compliments, some of those roses, and some of those acknowledgment notes? You bet.

What you sow, you reap

And this is not the reason I suggest you do it. That would be kind of selfish. No, it is enough fun, in and of itself, to do it and see and enjoy the reactions of people when you send those good things to them. But as a natural by-product of "What goes around comes around," you are likely to get some of it back, and at a time when you probably need it the most. It only takes 10 minutes per day to schedule in these little improvements, and the benefits will come back to you in spades.

INTERNET

www.kindnessinc.org/

Check out this web site to read about random acts of kindness and to share your own story. We could all use more kindness in our lives. Find out how you can help spread some!

Remember Orlando, the employee at the hotel? My involvement with him didn't end after my time management seminars. Orlando eventually left the hotel and I lost contact with him. I don't practice law very much these days because of my heavy seminar schedule. Besides, I would rather teach seminars than sue people. I don't take on new clients and serve only old clients in a few matters. A client called me a while back and asked me to represent him in a motor vehicle matter. We went to court and while standing in line, I looked behind me and spotted Orlando. I had not seen him for a few years, but we recognized each other and shook hands. He told me he was now the assistant bartender at an upscale hotel. His career was advancing nicely.

I asked what brought him to court this day as I did not imagine he had taken a day out of his busy schedule to learn about our court system. It seems he was stopped by the police and given tickets for driving without a license, operating an unregistered motor vehicle, and having no car insurance. Now, I am not going to make excuses for this behavior. Everyone should obey the law. But it was not like he was selling drugs illegally or engaging in some other harmful behavior.

■ **Small favors and acts of kindness** *are rewarded more often than you might think.*

Timely advice

Orlando was stressed out because well-meaning friends had given him some bad advice. He was told that he would have to pay a $500 fine this day and if he could not, he might have to go to jail. He was in a panic. I remembered how he had helped me when I needed a hand during my seminar, so I was happy to sit with him and give him a helping hand so that he did not get lost in a court system he was unfamiliar with.

I explained to Orlando that he needed to request a continuance first for 30 days; otherwise, he would probably wait around all day and the court would continue his case for a month anyway, and he would have wasted a day. Then, during that month, I told him he needed to get his driver's licence and get his car registered and insured. I told him that when he returned to court in a month, he could show the state's attorney that he held a valid driver's licence and that his car was properly insured. In many cases of this type, the state's attorney is usually willing to drop the charges, perhaps with the payment of a small fine.

Orlando was so relieved. I had given him the equivalent of $500 of legal advice – and I was pleased to be able to help. The point is, Orlando made the choice to spend 15 minutes of his time helping me set up chairs and tables for a seminar, even though it wasn't his job. What did he get back later on? Five hundred dollars' worth of legal advice. What goes around comes around.

Life is a series of choices. We all have choices about how we will act or not act, and those choices can have repercussions later on in life.

■ **The effort you make** *to help someone in need is never a waste of time.*

Many are concerned about how much their retirement fund will grow this year, whether it will grow at the rate of 12.1 percent or 12.6 percent. Forget about that! Consider a more generous bank, the bank of life. Send out good wishes, give compliments for a job well done, leave affectionate notes for your loved ones, and eventually it will all come back to you tenfold, often at times when you need it the most.

STEP 18:
LIST YOUR SEVEN LITTLE IMPROVEMENTS FOR TOMORROW

Build in one little improvement in each of your seven vital areas. Make each a little thing that will not take more than a few minutes to complete. Repeat the process every day to create about 2,500 little improvements in your life over the next 12 months.

■ **All the little improvements** *you make in your life eventually add up to a greater sense of well-being and happiness.*

A simple summary

✔ You can make about 2,500 improvements in your life in one year by building in one improvement each day in each of your seven vital areas.

✔ Investing only 10 minutes per day is all it takes to get the benefit from this tool.

✔ Don't get so caught up in the day-to-day business of living that you fail to acknowledge the efforts of others.

✔ It doesn't take a minute to send out good wishes to others – you will get them back tenfold.

✔ We are all presented with choices about how we live our lives; make sure that you take the right ones.

✔ Step 18 for organizing your life is to list your seven little improvements for tomorrow.

Chapter 19

The Personal Productivity System

THE PERSONAL PRODUCTIVITY SYSTEM is a chart I designed that brings together all the concepts discussed in this book. Let it be your daily guide to enhanced personal success. Use the chart as your daily checklist of building blocks to attend to and you will guarantee yourself a super day every day.

In this chapter...

✓ Climbing the personal productivity ladder

✓ The building blocks for increased personal productivity

✓ Where are you on the personal productivity ladder?

✓ Why the Olympians are good role models

✓ Step 19: Use the personal productivity system each day

IT IS POSSIBLE TO ACHIEVE YOUR PERSONAL BEST – JUST AIM HIGH AND STICK WITH IT

Climbing the personal productivity ladder

IF YOU FOLLOW THE STEPS *in the personal productivity system, the productivity you achieve at the top of the chart (see opposite) will be most effective in enhancing your daily success.*

Right now you probably spend most of your time at the top, at the production level. You're out there every day, doing what you do. But look at all the steps you can build in to magnify the success of your production. The key is to start each day at the bottom and work your way through each step to ensure super productivity every day. Let's take a closer look at each rung on the personal productivity ladder.

Daily planning

Increased personal productivity starts at the bottom of the chart, with the concept of daily planning. This means taking time each day, the night before, to plan out the most precious resource at your command – the next 24 hours. As a result of daily planning, you develop a road map for your tomorrow, having built in all the things you have to do and all the things you want do.

You also prioritize the tasks according to their importance using the prioritizing system of A for "crucial," B for "important," and C for "of little value." (By this point, you should have weeded out all the D tasks, "of no value," from your list; see Chapter 4 for more on prioritizing tasks.) Then you sub-prioritize within each category so that all of your scheduled tasks are laid out in a way that gives you the biggest bang for the buck for the next day, handling the more important matters first and leaving the less important matters for later.

■ **Daily planning** *is all about getting the most out of the next 24 hours – on or off the job.*

THE BUILDING BLOCKS FOR INCREASED PERSONAL PRODUCTIVITY

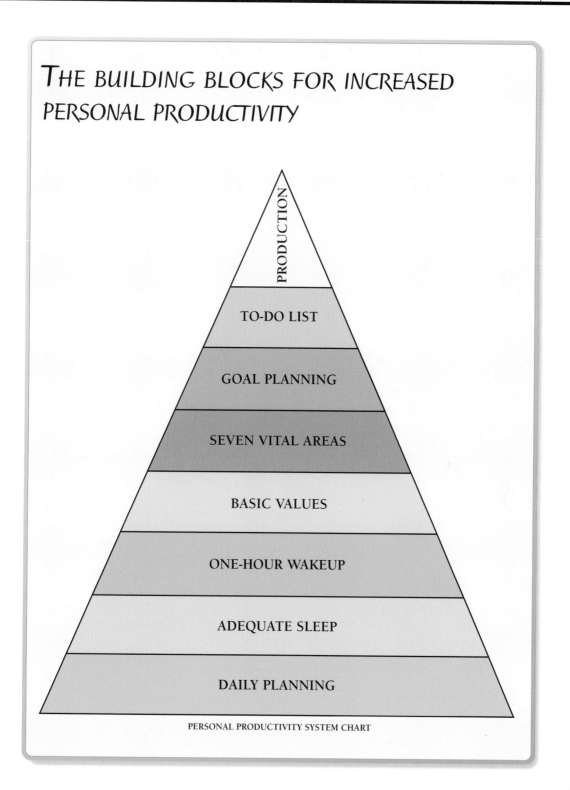

PERSONAL PRODUCTIVITY SYSTEM CHART

It's not what you leave undone that makes a difference; it's what you do accomplish that adds up to increased personal productivity.

This planning is done the night before so that you create a sense of certainty and control about the following day that you would not ordinarily have. That little voice in your head, whose job it is to pull together all the loose ends in your life, is silenced. The daily planning process takes those loose ends and puts them down on paper, where you can deal with them effectively.

INTERNET

www.sleepfoundation. org/nsaw/sleepiq99i.html

What's your sleep IQ? Find out by visiting this interesting site, run by the National Sleep Foundation.

Adequate sleep

The next step up the ladder is getting adequate sleep. Many people don't do any daily planning and experience highly stressful days as a result, always reacting to whatever is thrown at them instead of being in control of their day. Then, when bedtime arrives, they don't get the sleep that their body requires. And without a good night's rest, much of what we have discussed in this book can't work well for you. Studies show that many people are tired almost any time of the day because they don't get the quantity or quality of sleep they require. Experts say most people need between 6 and 8 hours of sleep per night to be able to function well the next day.

■ **Wake up!** *Without a good night's rest and a plan for the day, you'll feel less in control and more vulnerable to stress.*

You can help ensure that you get a good night's sleep by doing several things. During the last 30 minutes of your day, keep your thoughts positive. This will help you wind down from a stressful day. If you go to bed stressed, you have a tendency to carry that with you throughout your sleeping hours and it's what you will wake up with the following morning. Did you ever have a nasty argument with someone just before you went to bed? Perhaps you slammed down the phone or rolled over in bed in a huff? Ever notice how peacefully you slept afterwards, how refreshed you felt when you got up the next morning? I'll bet not. When the alarm went off in the morning, it was probably more like "Ding! Round 7!" You woke up still feeling upset and ready to continue the argument – that is, if you were able to get much sleep at all.

There's a lot of truth in the old expression "Don't let the sun set on your anger." Many people load up with negativity just before bedtime by watching the late-night news, which is inevitably filled with a lot of tragedy. Skip the news and fill the last 30 minutes of your day with something pleasant. Watch a rerun of your favorite comedy show, read a light novel, or have a pleasant conversation with that special person. Put yourself to sleep like a baby.

One-hour wakeup

Up another level on the personal productivity ladder is the one-hour wakeup. During the first 15 minutes of your waking day, do you ever notice how you are awake but not fully awake? You are putting one foot in front of the other, but you are not quite 100 percent alert. It's during this time that you are in what's called the *alpha state*. You are awake and conscious, but not at that fully awake state known as the beta level. We may go into this alpha state several times a day when we lose ourselves in daydreaming or just kicking back.

DEFINITION

*The **alpha state** is when your brain waves and physical cycles are slowed. Studies have shown that while in the alpha state we can as much as double our learning rate because our brain waves and physical cycles are most conducive to learning.*

■ **Start the day** *on a positive note – and you will be in a better frame of mind.*

Day-dreamer

Little kids are in the alpha state a lot. Perhaps it is near mealtime and you tell your 4-year-old, "Suzie, pick up your toys and come have supper. Suzie? Suzie!" and she is looking right at you and seemingly through you! We might say that Suzie is daydreaming, and she is. Little kids do this a lot because they have to learn a lot in a short period of time.

In the alpha state, you are at the highest level of learning receptivity. How do you learn? You learn by what you hear, see, smell, taste, and feel, and by what you think. A lot of people, not understanding how this works, get up first thing in the morning and turn on the news or pick up the newspaper to hear about all the terrible news from the night before, or they lay there in bed thinking, "What am I going to do about this project or that problem?" What is occurring during those first few minutes of your day is literally setting the stage for the kind of day you are going to have.

■ **Instead of rushing** *in the morning, get up an hour earlier, have a leisurely breakfast, and use the extra time – even if it's only 15 minutes – to read something you enjoy.*

Did you ever hear someone say, "Paula is having a bad day; she got out on the wrong side of the bed this morning"? Does Paula's bad day have anything to do with how Paula physically got out of the bed? Of course not. But it has everything to do with how she got out of bed mentally. I am asking you to take control of that. We all need a wakeup hour.

The wakeup hour

A lot of people use their first hour at work to wake up. Take advantage of this concept by getting up an hour earlier each day, before your normal wakeup time, to do three things:

1 Sit up on the edge of your bed so you aren't tempted to hit the snooze button on your alarm and go back to sleep. Get out of bed and brush your teeth, or whatever you need to do. Then, for the next 15 minutes, focus on the positive events in your life. Visualize yourself achieving a goal, getting that promotion, or traveling with your family. As long as you focus on the positive messages, the negative messages are blocked out.

2 For the second 15 minutes of this wakeup hour, do some inspirational reading. Read something that you find positive and uplifting. It need not be spiritual or religious in nature, although if you are comfortable with those materials, that would be fine. It may be an uplifting magazine article, a short story, or a biography. In doing so you are continuing to take control of that alpha state.

3 Then, during the final 30 minutes of this wakeup hour, go outside for a walk. Don't compromise safety, of course. If it's dark, carry a flashlight. If it's cold, dress accordingly. If you're afraid, get someone to walk with you. It need not be a vigorous walk; a stroll is just fine. While you are outside, focus on all of your senses. Smell things, see things, stop and listen to your world at that time of the morning. Feel the air and taste it, too. If you notice a leaf on the ground, stop and pick it up. Examine it. Delight in its beauty. When was the last time you stopped to study a leaf? See your world waking up while you collect your thoughts for the new day.

■ **Fine-tune your senses:** *look at the world around you and take the time to pay attention to small details of nature.*

It's worth it!

When you return at the end of a half-hour walk first thing in the morning, how will you feel? You will feel great! I have never met anyone who has followed this assignment to the letter and said it was a mistake. The hardest part, I know, is just simply doing it, dragging yourself out of bed. But try it! And the worse the weather, the more important it is to do this. If you can drag yourself out of bed on the coldest, stormiest morning, do the 15 minutes of positive visualization, followed by 15 minutes of inspirational reading, followed by a 30-minute walk, you will have accomplished a set of victories that is going to set the stage for the rest of the day.

What you have done in that one-hour wakeup is to take control of your mind, your body, and your environment – a triple reward. You have had an opportunity to nurture some, if not all, of your seven vital areas. You did some good things for your mental health with positive visualization, and the walk enhanced your physical health. Perhaps you take a family member along with you during the walk and enjoy some additional quality time together. You have read, so there is an intellectual component. You may run into a neighbor or two you never realized you had, for a social benefit. You got your thoughts in order, both work-related and spiritually, all within that one hour.

Trivia...

Did you ever have this experience? First thing in the morning, the radio is playing and perhaps you are not paying close attention to it. A song gets lodged in your head, and for the rest of the day, that song repeats itself in your head and you can't get the darn thing off your mind. What is going on in your day first thing in the morning can have a lasting effect on you all day even if you are not paying close attention to it.

■ **Share part of your** *1-hour wakeup with someone you love, and feel relaxed and happy instead of rushed and stressed.*

And what did it cost you? Just one hour of sleep that your body will adjust to. If your body does not adjust, plan to go to bed an hour earlier. You need to get up an hour before your normal wakeup time because you already have your routine in place. If you have not been in the habit of doing some or all of these things and you add new dimensions without factoring in more time to do them, your morning will be too rushed. You will have added stress to your life, not reduced it. Remember, the only way to get time for anything is to take the time.

Seventy-five percent of all heart attacks occur between the hours of 5 a.m. and 9 a.m. This time frame represents when most people wake up and start their day. Ninety percent of your car's engine wear occurs during the first few minutes of operation. The engine is cold, steel on steel. Until it warms up and gets lubricated, wear and tear occurs. We are like that car first thing in the morning. We need to warm up.

■ **If spending quality time** *with your family is one of your most basic values, plan for it!*

Basic values

Next up on the personal productivity system is basic values. Basic values are the foundation blocks upon which you build your life, the principles you feel strongly about. No amount of success can ever be permanent and lasting unless you act consistently with your unique set of basic values. Everyone has basic values, but few ever articulate them or write them down. So part of my permanent homework assignment for you is to work on your list of basic values and write them down.

■ **There's more to your day** *than making a living and holding down a good job. Attending a night-class to learn a new skill may satisfy other needs that are just as vital to maintaining a balanced life.*

What do you value?

Some of my basic values include spending quality time with my family, honesty, good health, humor, and loyalty. You may agree with some of these or perhaps you do not. Basic values are very personal things. Where do you find your basic values? One of the best places you will find them is during that inspirational reading you do each day during the second 15-minute period of your wakeup hour. As you read inspirational materials, concepts that you can identify with and add to your unique list will pop out at you.

To illustrate how important basic values are, let's look at "Quality time with family" as an example. Many people regard spending quality time with family as a basic value. Let's say, here is a person who has a job that requires 60 hours per week. In addition, this person attends classes three nights per week. He is also treasurer of his bowling league. All of these responsibilities translate into no time for family. There are only so many hours in the week.

People around this person often praise him for his achievements: "No one does it better than he does! Work, school, and the bowling league!" That person knows it should all feel good, but it doesn't. Why? Because there is no time left for his family – one of his basic values – and he feels an emptiness inside. If this emptiness grows he may abandon his course of action; in effect, sabotage his own productivity. But if he can identify the problem, he can make the adjustments to carve out the time he needs to spend with his family. The feeling of emptiness will diminish and his success will continue.

7 vital areas

Above basic values is the concept of the seven vital areas (see Chapter 2). Life is more than just making a living and doing a good job. As I've mentioned, life has seven dimensions to it, like a seven-legged table. If any one leg – never mind two or three – is longer than the rest, it can upset the entire table. While you may treat your social life differently than I treat my social life, and your intellectual life differently than I treat my intellectual life, we all have a social life, an intellectual life, and five other dimensions. You may not spend equal amounts of time in each area, or time every day in each area, but, in the long run, if you neglect any one area – never mind two or three – it will have a tendency to make your table – your life – wobbly and interfere with your ability to be successful and productive.

■ **All aspects of your life** – *social, professional, and personal – are interrelated. Be sure not to neglect any of them.*

Goal planning

The next level is goal planning, which is the idea of writing the book of your life backwards. We all walk about with the book of our life tucked under our arm. It has seven chapters in it, one for each of the seven vital areas, and every day you add a page to each chapter. You are literally writing the story of your life at this moment.

The last day of your life is the only day when you cannot change your life story.

"Time heals all wounds," as the saying goes. It doesn't matter what is broken in your life today, whether the problem lies in your relationships, finances, profession, or somewhere else. With time, you can fix it. But on the last day of your life, there is no time remaining to change your life story – it has been written.

■ **What is it** *that you are aiming for as your ultimate goal in life? A large family? A beautiful home? Decide what it is – and make sure you achieve it!*

How do you want each chapter to read on the last day of your life? What do you want to be able to say about your health? The time you've spent with your family? What you have accomplished financially? Your spirituality? You have a lot of control over how those chapters can end. Goal planning is deciding where you want to wind up on the last day of your life in each of your seven vital areas and then working backwards to determine what you have to do each year, each month, each week, and each day to get to where you want to go in life.

To-do list

Second from the top of the chart is the to-do list that you prepare each day to incorporate all the action steps you need to take to accomplish what you have to do and what you want to do the following day. It is your roadmap for the next day, giving you direction and control, keeping you from getting bogged down in all the little details.

Production

Finally, at the top of the chart, is production. This is the actual doing. All the talking, writing, and planning you do will not substitute for the doing. This is the area where you will spend the bulk of your time, but notice how small it is in relation to the entire personal productivity system. All those steps beneath it make that production meaningful and important.

Where are you on the personal productivity ladder?

WHERE DO MOST PEOPLE *fit in on the personal productivity system? Let's say for the sake of argument that virtually everyone, nearly 100 percent of people, are at the top level, production, doing the job, getting paid, and paying their bills. They are staying out of trouble and living day by day. There's nothing wrong with this. I offer no criticism.*

Don't put your head in the sand

How many people are at the next level, preparing a daily to-do list? About 70 percent of people use a to-do list most of the time and this is great. It helps them to focus on what has to be done and keep track of their responsibilities. But here is the problem. I have spoken to so many people over the years about coming to our time-management seminars and often I hear, "I don't need to go to a time-management seminar. I already use a to-do list. I already work with a clean desk. Nothing slips through the cracks here." My reply is, "Sounds like you're doing a good job of taking care of the 'have to'." "That's right. I get all the things done that have to be done."

Then I will ask, "Tell me a little about your family goals." "Family goals? What do family goals have to do with time management?" "Well, tell me a little about your basic values." "Basic values? What does that have to do with time management?" Build your house on a pit of gravel and see what happens.

■ **Being successful does not** *just mean having a tidy desk – you need to be focused and clear on the goals you have for all aspects of your life to achieve true success.*

The purpose of time management is more than just making up a good to-do list to administer the "have to's." It should also include taking time to do the "want to's."

How many people do a good job of goal planning? You would be hard-pressed to find someone who would speak against the concept of having personal goals in life. Try it. Go up to ten perfect strangers today and ask, "Should we have goals in life? Should anyone go through life without goals?" Almost everyone will tell you, "Have goals? Why, of course. You can't go through life without goals." Then ask this follow-up question, "What are your goals? Where are you going in your life in each of your seven vital areas?" I have found that only one in 20 will be able to answer that question. That is just 5 percent who will do the consistent hard work of actually identifying, planning, and implementing what they really want in their lives. Most give good lip service to the concept of goal planning, but few will actually follow through.

What are you aiming for?

Over the years, I have run into only a few people who have disagreed with the philosophy of the seven vital areas. But while there are few people who disagree with the concept of the seven vital areas, many people will tell me they don't have the time to create this balance in their lives. Their situation is such that they can only focus on one or two areas for now, perhaps just the financial and the professional areas. They have

recently taken on new responsibilities at work, are trying to develop a new sales territory, or are caught up in a job search that leaves them no time to devote to the other areas of their lives. But just as soon as they get over their current hump (like this is the last hump in life; did you ever have a time in your life when you didn't have humps or problems or challenges?), they will have time to create this balance in their lives.

■ **Goals are more** *than numbered items on a to-do list. They have the power to take you beyond the daily grind of doing the job, getting paid, and staying on top of your bills.*

They have it all backwards. Balance is not some reward that comes to us once we become successful. It is a necessary ingredient to become successful. If we are out of balance we create stress in our lives that interferes with our long-term, permanent success.

You can do a great job at work, but if you ignore your health and it fails, you risk losing all that short-term gain through illness. Likewise, if you ignore your family obligations, you might wind up in a divorce court.

Striving for perfection

Think for a moment about successful people you know, the people you really admire. Almost always they are in balance. Perfectly? No. There is no perfection in life. But by and large, over the long term, they are pretty well in balance first and that permits them to be successful.

How many people identify and live by their personal set of basic values? Very few. And while we all have basic values, few people take the time to think about them and write them down so they have a daily checklist to refer to, to ensure they are on the right path. Remember, no amount of success in your life will be permanent and lasting unless it is consistent with your unique set of basic values.

■ **Achieving a sense of** *balance is not as impossible as it seems – just keep working at it and you'll get there.*

■ **Balance has a huge** *impact on the long-term trajectory of a successful life. Your health is an essential ingredient of that balance. Don't neglect it.*

Quality is what counts

How about that one-hour wakeup? How many people practice this? So many people get up in the morning at the last possible moment (or a little later) and rush around just to get to work or to an appointment on time. They use the first hour or so at work to wake up and get up to speed.

How about adequate sleep? Many people get the quantity of sleep, the correct number of hours in bed, but they do not get the quality of sleep that they need. Their days are filled with stress, getting caught up in stuff, never getting to do the things they want to do, grabbing this fire hose or another to put out fires all day long. They fail to take the time to plan, and then put themselves to bed with negative thoughts and influences so that little voice in their head constantly reminds them about the loose ends in their life. Three out of four people, at any time of the day, will complain that they are flat-out tired. If you are not well-rested, it's tough to muster the energy to do the right things to have a productive day.

Trivia...

Did you ever notice that when you lose an hour in the morning you spend the rest of the day looking for it? It sets you behind the whole day.

Finally, at the bottom, is daily planning. Few people take the time to plan the most precious resource at our command, the next 24 hours. Their days are caught up just doing the job, all the while sacrificing the potential for what their lives could have been.

If you apply and follow the steps in the personal productivity system, the production you experience at the top will be nothing short of a gold-medal performance.

■ **The morning** is what sets the tone for your whole day, so don't start it by rushing and trying to beat the clock.

Why the Olympians are good role models

DO YOU LIKE TO WATCH the Olympic Games? If you're like me, you're in awe of what these champions do. They make their sport look so easy – but of course, we know how much skill is involved. I am a pretty good skier, but as I looked at the hill the Olympic skiers were traveling down, I knew it would have taken me 10 to 15 minutes to negotiate it. These Olympians were all speeding down that trail in just a few minutes and many were within hundredths of a second of each other. What do you think the skill differences are between first-place and last-place competitors? Probably very little. For the last-place finisher, it might have been an edge of a ski that caught or a moment's inattention that caused the skier to lose time and finish last.

■ **To become a competition-level** *athlete you need determination and dedication – valuable goals for any walk of life.*

Think like a winner

Do you think gold-medalist skier Tommy Moe woke up on the morning of his victory, opened the shades, stretched lazily, and said, "Hey, what's going on out here? A ski race? Medals? Gold, silver, and bronze? I dunno . . . maybe I'll try it, if I can rent some skis. Where do I go to sign up?" Of course not! All we saw the day he won was the production, coming down that mountain so flawlessly and then standing before the world to proudly accept that gold medal on behalf of his country and his achievement. What we did not see is all the planning, conditioning, practice, coaching, and sacrifice that led up to the day of the event. And without all of that, his production that day would not have secured him a gold medal and a place in history.

■ **Set aside time** *to write down your goals. With planning you can make greater strides toward achieving them.*

How many of us would like to have a gold-medal day, each and every day? Why would anyone compromise the gift of life for anything less? If we are to have a gold-medal day, every day, we have to earn it by preparing for it. That means living our lives on purpose, not by accident.

■ **Don't fall into the trap** *of living your life a day at a time, with no real sense of direction. Instead, live your life on purpose. Plan for things that are enjoyable and which enrich your days.*

STEP 19:
USE THE PERSONAL PRODUCTIVITY SYSTEM EACH DAY

Organize each day by setting aside some time the night before to attend to each step in the personal productivity system. This is not an expense, it is an investment. A little time spent doing this will make the next 24 hours significantly more productive and successful for you.

■ **Climbing the ladder** *of life can't be achieved overnight – it's something to strive for, one step at a time.*

A simple summary

✓ The building blocks for increased personal productivity will increase the success of the production you achieve each day.

✓ Most of your time is spent at the top at production, but the other steps enhance that production.

✓ Set yourself goals in all aspects of your life, giving it a sense of purpose.

✓ Go up the personal productivity ladder step by step to build a super day.

✓ The Olympians are good role models as we strive to make every day a gold-medal day.

✓ Step 19 for organizing your life is to use the personal productivity system each day.

Chapter 20

Practices for Your Personal Life

Y OU NEED TO DO A GOOD JOB of not only organizing your work life but your personal life as well. You can use the tools from this book to get more quality time with your family, be better organized, and ensure your continuous improvement in this rapidly changing world. So let's get personal.

In this chapter...

✓ Make time for your family and friends

✓ Schedule maintenance

✓ Organize your home

✓ Job transition tips

✓ Continuous personal improvement

✓ Step 20: Schedule time for family, maintenance, and organizing your home

Make time for your family and friends

ONE OF MY SEMINAR STUDENTS who was a very busy salesman asked me, "What is the best way to take my four-year-old daughter on vacation this year?" I thought about that for a minute and replied, "You take her now, while she is four years old." If you don't take a four-year-old on vacation, you can wait until she is a five-year-old, and that is nice. But you'll never have a second chance at taking that four-year-old if you don't do it now.

■ **There are lots of ways** of staying in touch with loved ones who live far away. Schedule regular contact – even if it is just a phone call.

So many wonderful opportunities to make lifelong memories with our family and friends slip by because we simply do not take the time to make them happen. Here are a few of the things I have done to create those memories.

The Sunday phone calls

When they were alive, my parents lived in another state and I did not get to see them as often as I would have liked. The same was true of my sister, who lived 3,000 miles away. Time would go by and my phone would ring. It might be my mother on the other end, reminding me that we hadn't talked for over 6 weeks, and that the telephone works both ways.

Don't fail to stay in touch – it can make you feel guilty. But how easy is it for the time to slip by – a week, then a month – without staying in touch with those you love?

I decided I needed to do better. I started scheduling a phone call to my parents and to my sister on a Sunday as an action item on my to-do list. When the call was done, I would schedule the next phone call I planned to make to them, perhaps the following Sunday. I would also do this for my friends who lived out of town and who I did not see frequently. Repeating this simple process kept me in touch with the people I care about; whereas before, time would slip by and I would forget.

A date with Dad

My wife and I have four kids. They are mostly grown-up now and have started lives and careers of their own.

To enhance the quality of our time together, we started the "Date with Dad" program early on. Once in the fall and once in the spring, I would set a date with each of my kids for just the two of us to go out some evening to spend time together. It would typically be a school night, which made it all the more special. Each child could pick the restaurant he or she wanted to go to and afterwards we might go to the shopping mall or stop somewhere for an ice-cream.

It was no big event, really, just a couple of hours together, one-on-one with each of my kids. And it was not 2 hours of "How come you're not doing your homework?" talk either. They heard enough of that already. It was just 2 hours with no agenda, a time to talk about whatever we wanted and to create some memories. I did that four evenings each fall and four evenings each spring, eight each year for 12 years. I spent nearly 100 evenings one-on-one with my kids over the years. It was not the only thing we did but it was one more neat thing that we remember.

Trivia...
When my children were growing up, I was away a lot at meetings in the evening or traveling on business like a lot of fathers. The time we had together was precious, although we always wish we had had more of it. Therefore, I was always looking for ways to create more quality time.

■ **Seize the opportunity** *to spend quality time with your family, otherwise you may lose the moment forever.*

■ **Your kids will enjoy** – *and always remember – a weekend trip where you focus on them exclusively. Schedule the time for an adventure away from everyday life and spend some quality time with your kids..*

The point is, I did not wait until the time came to me. I took the time. I scheduled it with the same sense of importance that I would schedule a business meeting.

One other fun thing I did with the kids over the years was schedule a "Weekend with Dad". I have two girls close in age and two boys close in age. Once in the fall and once in the spring, I would schedule a weekend with the two girls and another weekend with the two boys. (My wife would be with the other pair for her "Weekend with Mom".) It would be an all-weekend affair. They kids could pick where they wanted to go. My girls were older than the boys and, of course, more sophisticated, so they would want to go to a hotel for a nice lunch. My boys liked camping or boating. We would leave on a Saturday morning and enjoy an overnight adventure. We had 2 full days of making memories and enjoying each other's company. This time with my children would never have happened if I hadn't scheduled it.

Some time for your spouse

Here are a few ideas on taking time for your spouse or significant other:

1 *Daily phone call:* I travel a lot, and when I'm not traveling, I'm in my office. But wherever I am, I schedule a daily phone call to my wife. It's nothing special, just to check in and tell her that I love her. Hearing her return the sentiment always brightens my day.

2 *Weekend getaways:* This was especially valuable when we had our four growing kids at home. Twice a year, my wife and I would schedule a weekend getaway, ship the kids off to Grandma, and spend Friday night to Sunday afternoon together somewhere away from home. Maybe we would go to New York City, see a show, take in a movie, and enjoy a quiet dinner or two. There was no agenda and no arguing, just time together to enjoy each other the way we did before we got married.

3 *Date night:* As best we can, my wife and I set aside Friday or Saturday night for just the two of us, perhaps for a quiet dinner, a movie, or an afternoon at the golf course. No parties or going out with other couples. I'm often away on weekends, so we usually reserve a weeknight for our date night. There's only one way to make it happen. You have to make it happen.

4 *Surprise roses:* I send or bring home flowers for my wife from time to time, when there is no real occasion to commemorate and when she least expects it. I might even send some flowers to her at work. She enjoys them, and I do too.

5 *Love note:* I may leave one of my poems under her pillow or on the dashboard of her car before she goes to work ("Roses are red; Violets are blue; You're terrific; But so am I too!"). (I really do better than that!) I know my wife appreciates the thought, but it is also a regular helpful reminder to me of who she is and what she means to me.

As with your business responsibilities, to make it happen you must take the time to do it. Use your to-do list to schedule time to do things that will enhance your relationship with the people you love.

■ **With a little preparation** *you can enjoy holidays with your family – and still be on speaking terms when it's over!*

Scheduling time with family and friends

Similarly, you can schedule family and friends "fun time." Perhaps Wednesday evenings can be family night. The holidays are a time to see family and friends and a period of great joy for some, but a source of stress and frustration for others. None of us should be denied the true joys of each holiday season. On the next page you'll find some suggestions to help you control holiday stress and enjoy this time even more with your family and friends:

The holidays usually require more of our time for special preparations in addition to our regular routines and responsibilities. Many of us get caught short, running around at the last minute as we try to get everything done. The solution is to plan ahead and schedule these tasks and events with greater care. It always seems to get done sooner or later. Why not sooner, at your pace, without so much of the hassle?

1. *Delegate:* Trying to do it all may be an impractical goal that only serves to stress you out. Share the shopping, cooking, cleaning, and other responsibilities with others. You don't have to do everything yourself. There is only so much time in a day, and besides, people generally appreciate the opportunity to participate in the preparations.

2. *Get enough sleep:* During the holidays, with all the parties, preparations, shopping, gift wrapping, and cooking, it's easy to pay for the additional time required with your sleep time. Many people don't get enough sleep, so they get cranky and don't enjoy what they are doing as much. Not only that, they may not exactly be a pleasure to be around! Each of us has a different sleep quota that we require to feel rested. Especially during the busy holiday period, take the time for adequate sleep so that you have the energy to get into the full swing of things and enjoy the holidays as they unfold.

■ **If you're worried** *about gaining weight over the holidays, lose a few pounds beforehand, which may be less stressful than trying to lose it afterwards.*

3. *Don't overindulge:* The holidays are a time when it's easy to overindulge in eating and drinking. The problem is, we pay for it later and sometimes sooner. A little advance planning might help as well. For example, if you know that you always gain five pounds over the holidays, make it a point to drop five pounds before the holiday season. Many people find it is easier and less stressful to lose that additional weight before rather than after the holidays.

4. *Set a financial budget:* We tend to want to be generous and when shopping it is easy to fall prey to "impulse buying" and go all out with the credit cards. Then we experience the post-holiday blues when the bills arrive in January. Plan what you will spend before you go to the stores and stick to those budget amounts.

5. *Don't overload:* This is not the last holiday period you will enjoy. You can't do everything, but you can do and enjoy the most important things. Sure, you will do more now than at other times during the year. Have a grand time, a memorable holiday season. Just don't try to do it all. Save something for next year.

6. *Enjoy the journey:* Don't "dread" any part of it – the shopping, wrapping, cooking, cleaning, etc. Find happiness in all of it. Enjoy it all. Some people place all their eggs in one basket. If all the celebration and the joy are scheduled for one night, perhaps Christmas Eve, what happens if it's a disappointment? The whole season is a bust. Enjoy everything leading up to the "big night" and enhance the quality and your level of enjoyment of the entire season.

Schedule maintenance

A BIG TIMESAVER is to make sure that everything – from the car to the computer to your health – is properly maintained so that you operate smoothly and without breakdown. Emergency breakdowns cost a lot of time and most can be prevented with planned maintenance.

The things you own

Take your car for scheduled maintenance. Get the oil changed regularly. It will be less expensive in the long run and more reliable for your use. When things start making funny noises, get them checked out right away.

All of a sudden one day, my home computer started to make a strange whirring sound. Over the next day or so it got louder. I took it to my local computer repair place and was told a fan was wearing out and "for a nominal $50" it could be fixed. I was also told that if it was not fixed immediately, my hard drive might well be damaged permanently, causing it to lose stored data. As the saying goes, "A stitch in time saves nine."

Have your heating and cooling systems checked out periodically, too. If there's a problem, fix it right away so it doesn't mushroom into a much larger one.

A tune-up for you

Keep yourself in good shape as well. Schedule an annual physical with your doctor. See your dentist regularly. Eat right and exercise often. Take appropriate vitamins. Laugh a lot, too. Don't forget the importance of giving your body enough rest. Most of us seem to get by comfortably with about eight hours of sleep each night. That might be high or low for you. Whatever you need, make sure you schedule it.

■ **Make sure you** *look after yourself! Have enough rest so that you have enough energy to live your life to the full.*

Don't deprive yourself of sleep. Many people complain throughout the day that they are flat-out tired from lack of sleep. They may stay up late watching their favorite television show or surfing the Internet; then, the next day, they cannot be as productive as they need to be. Things take longer to get done and much does not get done.

A tune-up for the family

Encourage the rest of your family to stay in good shape, too. A chain is no stronger than its weakest link. If one family member gets sick, it has an effect on the entire family's productivity. Take after-dinner walks with your spouse or partner, toss a ball around with your kids, play fetch with the dog, or take up a new sport as a family. Not only are you and your family keeping healthy, you're sharing quality time as well.

Organize your home

You don't have to strive for a perfectly neat and orderly home environment (especially if you have kids or pets!). However, if you have a degree of organization, a command of the clutter will help you to get more done. Just making some simple changes will yield big results.

A clean work area

Just as you would want to work with a clean desk at work, use clean work areas at home – whether it be the kitchen, the hobby room, the bathroom, or the garage. Remember the advice I gave you in Chapter 12. If it's out of sight, it's out of mind. And the reverse of that is true as well: when it's in sight, it's in mind, and you cannot help being distracted by it.

■ **Good organization** *is just as important at home as it is at work. Keeping your work area in the kitchen clear of messes, for example, helps make cooking and preparing meals all the more enjoyable.*

As best you can, put things in their place in drawers or storage bins or hanging up where they need to be. It will be less time-consuming to locate these items when you need them if they are where they should be in the first place. You can waste a lot of time looking for something like a pair of slippers or a roll of tape because you forgot where you left it, or it's buried under some other stuff.

Keep your car keys and other important keys in one place, such as on a hook by the door, so you'll always know where to find them.

Managing important papers

Organize all of your important papers in one location, such as a filing cabinet. Use separate hanging folders for each category. For example, you might have a folder for the certificate of title for your car or other vehicle information, one for retirement information, one for wills, one for insurance policies, one for investments, one for paid bills, one for cancelled checks and bank statements, one for tax returns, and anything else you need to keep track of. Let family members know where to find these papers in case of an emergency. It's wise to keep copies of important documents such as wills in a safety deposit box at your bank.

Clean it out and give it away

We all tend to accumulate stuff. Things we buy and gifts we receive add to the clutter and disorganization of many households. Set aside time every now and again – maybe a Saturday a couple of times a year – to go through your stuff and discard the things you no longer use. Get rid of the things that are broken that can't be easily fixed. Discard or donate to charity any toys your kids have outgrown and don't play with anymore. Clean out your closets and donate to the Salvation Army or Goodwill any clothes that no longer fit or that you don't wear anymore. If the clothing or other items are in good condition, offer them to people who may need them.

■ **Effective management also** *applies to the clutter you don't know what to do with at home: Recycle it, give it away to a thrift shop, or donate it to a community project.*

Master grocery list

A lot of time is wasted by making multiple trips to the grocery store. Many people draw up a big shopping list once a week but find themselves running back and forth to the grocery store 2 or 3 times a week for items not on the list. Make up a master grocery list and hang it on the refrigerator at the beginning of the week. As you run out of items, add them to the list. If you think you would like to have pasta for dinner on Sunday, put it on. Look ahead to the next week and see what else you might require. If you're having a friend over for dinner, for example, you might want to pick up a dessert or that special brand of coffee you know your guest likes.

> ### Trivia...
> Somebody suggested an interesting practice to me. Twice a year he goes through his stuff and gets rid of anything he has not used in the last 2 years. No matter what it is – clothing, an electronic gadget, or a piece of furniture – if he hasn't used it in 2 years, he feels it is unlikely he will ever use it and he passes it on to someone else who might have a current use for it. I can't quite bring myself to follow such a neat policy but I think it's a good idea.

Job transition tips

TODAY, THE AVERAGE PERSON *changes jobs every 3 years. Job change is one of the less desirable tasks we must perform in life; for many, it's right up there with a root canal. Why? Because we don't like rejection. We don't like to be judged. Just as we wouldn't be too good at golf if we played it only once every 3 years, if we go through the job-seeking task every 3 years or so, we probably are not going to be comfortable with our skills.*

There are many resources at the library and on the Internet to help you in networking, sending resumés, and interview preparation. Let's discuss here how to do all that in half the time.

When I received my degree in accounting in 1970, our graduation speaker told us we ought to plan on having three or four jobs in our careers. When my daughter graduated from college just a few years ago, her graduation speaker predicted that they ought to plan on having three or four different careers in their work lives.

■ **There are so many** *time-saving resources to help you out when you are job hunting – the library and the Internet are just two of them.*

The employment campaign

First, if you were out of work tomorrow, either involuntarily or by choice, how long would you estimate it would take you to find employment? We never know for sure, but it's important to form an educated guess so that we know what we are up against. To find out, talk to several people who have recently gone through the same type of job search you are about to do. Ask them how long it took to secure their new positions. You will quickly get a sense of the average length of time it is likely to take. Let's assume that for your objective, in your industry, at your skill level, and in your desired geography, it takes about 90 days to successfully complete the new employment campaign. Certainly you may beat those averages or you may take considerably longer, but it is useful to know a range of probability.

Next, analyze the three building blocks for getting a new job. It starts with resumés, targeted to specific recipients. This leads to interviews done well. Complete enough good interviews and you will receive job offers.

Let's assume you would like to have three job offers to consider. How many interviews does it take, in your area, to get 1 offer? Find out by talking to several people who have recently secured the type of job you want

■ **Although it may take** *a while to find out how many interviews are needed to get the job you want – the time you invest in research will pay off.*

and ask how many interviews they conducted and how many job offers resulted. Talk with hiring authorities for your type of position and ask how many interviews they typically conduct to generate one offer.

Let's assume you have determined that it takes, on average, five interviews to get one job offer. If your goal is three job offers, that means you need to create about 15 interviews.

How many resumés does it take, on average, to generate 1 interview at your job objective level? Don't know? Most don't. How do you find out? Again, talk to several people who have recently secured the type of job you want and ask how many resumés they had to send out to secure one interview. Talk with hiring authorities for your type of position and ask how many resumés they typically generate for your type of job and how many interviews they extend. Let's assume you have determined that it requires ten resumés to generate one interview. If your goal is 15 interviews, that means you need to send out about 150 resumés during your campaign.

Job hunting is a sales operation — you are selling yourself. Like any good salesperson, you need to know where you're going and what it will take to get there. If you don't know, the temptation is to simply work hard, not really knowing how far along you truly are on the path to that new position. Lacking a clear direction builds in stress and fatigue, and fosters discouragement.

■ **In most jobs** *you don't necessarily get ahead by working longer hours. The same is true of job hunting. Without a clear objective you may lose sight of the path you should be taking to get where you want to go.*

Having determined that it takes, on average, 3 months to complete the job-search campaign, knowing that you need to circulate 150 well-placed resumés, you now have a monthly goal of 50 resumés or approximately two per business day. So what's your goal tomorrow? Send out two targeted resumés. Does that get the new job for you? Probably not. But when you go to bed tomorrow night, you know you have taken the right first step on this journey. A week later, you have sent out ten resumés, received three rejection letters, and no interviews. Are you discouraged? No, you're on target. You're developing the quantity to get to the quality. You understand your numbers.

So, how do you get a job in half the time? Double the daily output of targeted resumés sent from two per day to four per day. You will "expose" yourself in the quantity necessary in half the time and increase the probability of getting the required quantity of interviews and resulting job offers in significantly less time.

Continuous personal improvement

AS YOU GO FORWARD in this new Information Age, more and more of your personal and professional success will be in direct relationship to three key skill areas that you need to continuously improve upon. Together they form what I call the "productivity triangle." These three skill areas are:

1. The ability to better manage your time, your most valuable resource to leverage your success.

2. The ability to absorb greater quantities of information each day.

3. The ability to express your ideas and give information to others, both orally and in writing.

Let's take a closer look at each area.

1.) Time management

Time is your most precious resource. You have 24 hours each day, 7 days a week, for a total of 168 hours per week. You probably already have too much to do and not enough time in which to do it. You are working longer hours today and have less leisure time than you did 10 years ago. This is going to continue unless you take action now to reverse that trend in your life. You can no longer continue to work harder. You are running out of time to do that. You have to develop ways to work smarter, to be able to get more done in less time, with less stress, in both your work and personal life. You need to continue your education in time management and organizational skills. Practice the techniques outlined in this book and reread them often.

■ **With the same number** *of hours there have always been in a day, but with so much more to do and accomplish in each of them, all of us can benefit from time management.*

2.) Speed reading

Today, you probably get more information tossed at you in one day than your great-grandparents received in a lifetime. Knowledge is power. If the flow of information coming at you is increasing, then without increasing your ability to absorb it, you are actually receiving less and less of what you need to know to compete and succeed in today's world. You are actually falling behind.

The average person spends about 2 hours a day reading at a rate of about 200 words per minute. If you can double your reading speed, you can read and absorb twice as much information in the same amount of time or cut your daily reading time in half, saving an hour a day, every day. And when you absorb more information, you will enjoy more success. Make it an important goal, a high priority, to complete a speed-reading course so that you can absorb information more rapidly, for your success.

3.) Communications skills

It is said that the thing we fear second only to the death of a loved one is public speaking! I know it because I have been a full-time professional speaker for over 20 years and have taught personal communication skills to thousands. But the ability to comfortably and effectively communicate information and ideas to others is the final key to your success. Whether it is one-on-one or to a group, or some writing you must do, if you feel intimidated and can't express your thoughts and ideas clearly, you will do less of it and thereby limit your success.

Expressing your ideas comfortably, confidently, and without fear can be learned. Make it a high priority to enroll in a public-speaking program and a writing skills program to increase your ability and confidence in expressing your ideas to others.

These three skills work together. Improvement in one area helps you in the other two. If you can absorb information more quickly, you will save time and have more to offer others. If you can manage your time more effectively, you will get more done in less time, you will be able to acquire more knowledge, and you will have more time to communicate that to others. And if you can more comfortably and easily express your ideas and share your knowledge with others, you will get more information back and advance your success in less time.

Combining all three skills areas will give you a synergistic payback. Improving these three skill areas will give you a quantum leap and a continuous boost in your success, both professionally and personally.

INTERNET

www.toastmasters.org

This is the home page of Toastmasters International, a well-known organization that can help you become more comfortable with public speaking and improving your communication skills in general. This web site gives you information on becoming a member, finding a Toastmasters club near you, speaking tips, and more.

STEP 20:
SCHEDULE TIME FOR FAMILY, MAINTENANCE, AND ORGANIZING YOUR HOME

Take a close look at each area of your personal life to see how you can improve it. If you need to spend more time with your family or friends, schedule it. If you need to organize your home so that you can be more productive, make that a to-do task also. Taking the time to organize your personal life will pay off later, in both greater satisfaction and improved productivity.

■ **With a little organization,** *you can spend more time with your family and be as productive and successful as you want to be in your career.*

A simple summary

✔ Make time for your family and friends. If you don't take the time, you'll never get it.

✔ Schedule maintenance for your things and for you – it is best to fix problems before they become larger problems.

✔ Organize your home and take command of clutter.

✔ Job transition tips will help you to get your next job in a lot less time.

✔ Continuous personal improvement is the foundation of your continued success.

✔ Step 20 for organizing your life is to schedule time for family, maintenance, and organizing your home.

ORGANIZING YOUR LIFE: THE STEPS

YOU HAVE READ THROUGH THIS BOOK, and you know how to *manage* your time effectively and organize your life efficiently. Despite having implemented many of the changes suggested here, there may be occasions when you need a quick *reminder* of some of the fabulous  facts you have learned, or you may simply want to brush up on those areas that need attention.

To help you out, the following pages provide an at-a-glance *reference* of the steps listed in the main part of the book. Refer again to the specific hints and tips that will help you make changes in your life, and decide what action you need to take to make these concrete. Don't forget what you have learned in these pages: organizing your life is for life!

USE YOUR NEW ORGANIZATIONAL SKILLS TO GET THE MOST OUT OF YOUR LIFE

Refresher Guide

TO FOLLOW ARE THE STEPS *that will help you on your way to achieving a better organized life. This is intended to be a quick guide to the top tips you have learned in this book, so refer back to specific chapters as often as you need to.*

1 RATE YOUR PRODUCTIVITY FROM 1 TO 10

As we quantify certain things it may help us to understand them better. On a scale of 1 ("lousy") to 10 ("perfect"), rate your productivity. Don't rate yourself in just the work environment; take into account your productivity throughout the entire day.

2 COMPLETE THE BALANCE WHEEL

Rate your current performance, as of this day, in each of your seven vital areas on the balance wheel, from 1 ("lousy") to 10 ("perfect"). It's a good idea to make several copies of the chart before you fill it in so you can use it for other days too.

3 MAKE UP YOUR TO-DO LIST

Using your tool of choice, paper or electronic, make up your own to-do list. List all of the things you have to do and all of the things you want to do over the next 24 hours. You may develop a list of a dozen items or even more – the more things you can list, the better. Don't feel too overwhelmed!

4 PRIORITIZE YOUR TO-DO LIST

Your to-do list is a compilation of everything you have to do and want to do. In order to get the maximum done in the time available, prioritize the list so you focus on the most important items.

5 CREATE YOUR CALENDAR OF SCHEDULED EVENTS

On a full-month-at-a-glance calendar record all your appointments and scheduled events. Whenever you schedule an appointment or event, write it down on your calendar immediately, so you don't forget it. Keep the calendar with you and refer to it often.

6 RUN YOUR CRISIS MANAGEMENT LOG

Schedule a time to run your crisis management log for a 2-week period. Study the results to see if you can detect any patterns, and then take corrective action to prevent those crises from reoccurring.

7 START USING THESE USEFUL TOOLS

Get a supply of 3 x 5 index cards and write down all the things that slip through the cracks. Make up birthday, anniversary, and gift-giving lists. Assemble your telephone directory.

8 LIST YOUR PROCRASTINATED ITEMS AND SOLUTIONS

Review the items on your to-do list that you have been carrying forward, that you have been procrastinating about doing. Make a positive decision to get these items done.

9 DECIDE WHAT TASKS YOU COULD HAVE DELEGATED TO OTHERS

Review what you have done in the last couple of weeks and determine which items you could have delegated to others that would have freed up your time for more important matters.

10 DECIDE WHAT AND TO WHOM YOU CAN DELEGATE

Take a look at all of your appointments and scheduled events coming up. Review all the discretionary items built into your to-do lists. Look at every item and ask yourself if doing the task makes the best use of your time. If it is, plan to do it. If not, try to delegate it to free your time for more important things.

11 DECIDE WHAT FUTURE MEETINGS YOU CAN SKIP

Look at your future appointments and scheduled events. Review each and ask yourself whether the meeting is necessary and, if so, whether you need to attend. Do what you can to get out of attending those meetings that are unnecessary.

12 SCHEDULE A DATE TO CLEAN UP YOUR WORK AREA

Decide when you will clean up your disorganized work area. Enter this task as an action statement on your to-do list for that day.

13 GETTING A HANDLE ON YOUR PAPERWORK

Set aside a couple of hours to review all of the paper you have been receiving recently, including memos, faxes, junk mail, e-mails, and voice mail. Identify the items that are of little or no value and commit to taking action to stop the flow of these unwanted communications.

14 SCHEDULE YOUR TIME LOG

Set a date to begin and run your time log for several days. Analyze your results and take corrective steps to eliminate the time-wasters in your life.

15 KEEP A LOG OF WHO YOU INTERRUPT

Keep a log of whenever you interrupt another person for a week or two. After gathering this data, go through each entry and decide which interruptions were of the A (crucial) or B (important) variety and which were of the C (of little value) or D (of no value) variety. Take actions to avoid bringing C and D interruptions to others.

16 KEEP AN INTERRUPTIONS LOG

Run an interruptions log for 3 to 5 days and analyze your results so you can find ways to reduce some of the C and D interruptions in your day, giving you more time to handle more of the A and B tasks on your to-do list. Run the log every few months so you can assess your interruptions and take corrective steps.

17 SCHEDULE YOUR LIFE IMPROVEMENT CHART

Set a date for sitting down to work on your life improvement chart. Begin the process of leveraging the control you have over your future.

18 LIST YOUR SEVEN LITTLE IMPROVEMENTS FOR TOMORROW

Build in one little improvement in each of your seven vital areas. Make each a little thing that will not take more than a few minutes to complete. Repeat the process every day to create about 2,500 little improvements in your life over the next 12 months.

19 USE THE PERSONAL PRODUCTIVITY SYSTEM EACH DAY

Organize each day by setting aside some time the night before to attend to each step in the personal productivity system. This is not an expense, it is an investment. A little time spent doing this will make the next 24 hours significantly more productive and successful for you.

20 SCHEDULE TIME FOR FAMILY, MAINTENANCE, AND ORGANIZING YOUR HOME

Take a close look at each area of your personal life to see how you can improve it. Taking the time to organize your personal life will pay off later, in both greater satisfaction and improved productivity.

To-do lists

Must do	Completed

Must do	Completed

Further reading

All I Really Need to Know I Learned in Kindergarten
Robert Fulgrum, Random House, 1989

Chicken Soup for the Soul
Jack Canfield and Mark Victor Hansen, Heath Communications, 1995

Crisis Management: Planning for the Inevitable
Steven Fink, IUniverse.com, 2000

Development First: Strategies for Self-Development
David B. Peterson, Personnel Decisions International, 1995

Dig Your Well Before You're Thirsty
Harvey Mackay, Doubleday, 1999

Don't Sweat the Small Stuff
Richard Carlson, Hyperion, 1997

Dr. Weisinger's Anger Work-Out Book
Henchie D. Weisinger, William Morrow & Co., 1985

Getting It Right: How Working Mothers Successfully Take Up the Challenge of Life, Family, and Career
Laraine T. Zappery, Pocket Books, 2001

Good Things for Organizing, Vol. 2
Martha Stewart, Crown Publishing Group, 2001

How to Make Meetings Work
Michael Doyle and David Straus, Berkley Publishing Group, 1993

How to Win Friends & Influence People
Dale Carnegie, Simon & Schuster, 1982

I Could Do Anything If I Only Knew What It Was: How to Discover What You Really Want and How to Get It
Barbara Sher and Barbara Smith, DTP, 1995

Leadership Begins With You: 3 Rules to Transform Your Job into a Career
Mary Morgan Riley, Perigee, 2001

Love the Work You're With: Find the Job You Always Wanted Without Leaving the One You Have
Richard C. Whiteley, Henry Holt & Company, 2001

Making a Living Without a Job: Winning Ways for Creating Work That You Love
Barbara J. Winter, Bantum Doubleday Dell Publishing, 1993

Release the Power Within People for Astonishing Results
Ken Blanchard, Jon Carlos, and Alan Randolph; Berrett-Koehler Publishers, 1999

Super-Memory–Super Student: How to Raise Your Grades in 30 Days
Harry Lorayne, Little Brown & Co., 1990

Take Time for Your Life: A Personal Coach's Seven-Step Program for Creating the Life You Want
Cheryl Richardson, Broadway Books, 1999

10 Days to More Confident Public Speaking
Lenny Laskowski, Warner Books, 2001

The Art of Growing Up: Simple Ways to Be Yourself at Last
Veronique Vienne, Clarkson Potter, 2000

The 80/20 Principle: The Secret of Achieving More With Less
Richard Koch, Doubleday & Company, 1999

The Greatest Salesman in the World
Og Mandino, Bantam Doubleday Dell Publishing Group, 1974

The Life Strategies Workbook: Exercises and Self-Tests to Help Change Your Life
Philip C. McGraw, Hyperion, 2000

The Power of Positive Thinking
Norman Vincent Peale, Simon & Schuster, 1989

The Procrastinator's Handbook: Mastering the Art of Doing It Now
Rita Emmett, Walker & Co., 2000

The Road Less Traveled
M. Scott Peck, Simon & Schuster, 1997

The 7 Habits of Highly Effective People
Stephen Covey, Fireside, 1990

The Ten Commandments of Goal Setting
Gary Ryan Blair, The Goals Guy, 1999

The Values Book: Teaching 16 Basic Values to Young Children
Tamera Bryant, Pam Schiller, and Pamela Byrne Schiller, Gryphon House, 1998

Think & Grow Rich
Napoleon Hill, Fawcett Books, 1990

What Color is Your Parachute? 2001: A Practical Manual for Job-Hunters & Career Changers
Richard Nelson Bolles, Ten Speed Press, 2000

Who Moved My Cheese?
Spencer Johnson, Simon & Schuster, 1998

Work Smart: The 250 Smart Moves Your Boss Already Knows
Marci Taub, Princeton Review, 1998

You Can Heal Your Life
Louise L. Hay, Hay House, Inc., 1999

Web sites

AT THE TIME OF WRITING, all of the web sites listed here were state-of-the-art. But web sites come and go very quickly. Therefore, while every effort has been made to ensure the accuracy of the Internet information published here and elsewhere in the book, please accept my apologies if a site you are interested in no longer exists. Furthermore, the publisher cannot accept responsibility for the information contained within these sites, or any links from them. Happy surfing!

www.balancetime.com
This time-management super site offers free articles, tips, and an online stress test to help you easily organize your life.

www.carleton.ca/~tpychyl
Carleton University in Ottawa, Ontario, Canada, maintains this site as the Procrastination Research Group. It's a compilation of information and research on procrastination from all over the world.

www.cmha.ca
The Canadian Mental Health Association and its various divisions offer a stress test and workshops to help deal with stress in the workplace.

www.crisisexperts.com
If you really want to get into the heart and soul of crisis management and explore some unique approaches, visit this site, run by the Institute for Crisis Management.

www.cyberworking.com
This site, run by Cyber Working Moms, provides tips and resources for working mothers (and dads!).

www.daytimer.com
Visit this site to find out more about the full range of Day-Timer products, contact information, and ordering forms.

www.the-dma.org
Contact this site, run by the Direct Marketing Association, to request that your name and address be removed from mailing lists.

www.excite.com/careers
This career site, run by the Excite search engine, offers career resources and tips.

www.financesource.net/index.html
Check out this site for a complete guide to personal finance on the Internet.

www.get-a-grip-on-your-life.com
This site offers tips and information for getting control of your life, as well as links to many health-related topics.

www.getorganizednow.com
Browse this site for a lot of tips and ideas to help you organize your home, your office, and your life.

www.iavoa.com

A whole new profession of virtual assistants is emerging to help you get more done in less time, through delegation. The International Association of Virtual Office Assistants (IAVOA) site discusses the benefits of using virtual assistants and provides a directory of members.

www.ljlseminars.com

This well-organized site is packed with tips and information about how to improve your public speaking skills.

www.mybookmarks.com

Check this site to take advantage of a free service that allows you to list and bookmark your favorite web sites and access them from anywhere on the Internet.

www.neffzone.com/prolinks

Personal productivity resources on the Web are featured here.

www.pueblo.gsa.gov

This site offers consumer information center sponsored by the United States government that offers tons of useful free stuff to enrich your organized life.

www.sleepfoundation.org/nsaw/sleepiq99i.html

In a 1999 US survey, 83 percent of adult Americans failed the NSF Sleep IQ Test. Find out your sleep IQ by visiting this site.

www.the-work-at-home.com/newsletter/subscribe.htm

Subscribe to "At Home Working News" for free to get answers to your questions on working from home.

www.toastmasters.org

The site of Toastmasters International offers tips on improving your public speaking skills, as well as information on becoming a member and finding a club near you.

www.topica.com/lists/timemanagement

This site offers a free "Timely Time Management Tips" newsletter sent to you via e-mail with easy tips to get more done in less time.

www.usatoday.com/careers/news/news007.htm

A list of the 100 best companies for working moms (and dads).

www.wellweb.com

The Wellness home page offers lots of excellent health tips.

www.wordsmith.org/awad

Sign up and A Word A Day will send a word and its definition to you each day. It's a simple way to improve your vocabulary.

www.workopolis.com

Contact Canada's biggest job site for advice from professionals, job opportunities, and career resources.

A simple glossary

Address book
An addition to your daily calendar that contains important names, addresses, phone numbers, and other valuable information.

Agenda
A list of items to be covered at a meeting.

Anticipation
The ability to refer to one source each night and review your appointments, scheduled events, and to-do list items and assess what can be done to make each event run smoothly and productively.

Appointment
A commitment to a certain date and time, whether business or personal. *See also* scheduled events.

Balancing your life
The understanding that your life comprises many dimensions, and that long-term success requires that these need to be balanced.

Basic values
Core beliefs, held in the highest regard that govern your daily conduct.

Birthday and anniversary lists
A simple way to track important dates so that they are not overlooked.

Clean desk
The notion of working with one item at a time and putting away the rest.

Context
Scheduling appointments and events, taking into account what precedes and follows them, considering your work habits.

Crisis management
What occurs when a deadline sneaks up on you and robs you of all choice.

Crisis management log
A simple tool you can use to catalog crises as they occur, enabling you take corrective action to prevent their reoccurrence.

Crucial item
A task of the highest priority.

Curse of perfectionism
The goal of trying to do things to perfection, which is impossible and leads to stress and frustration.

Daily planning
Time set aside each day to take control of a precious resource – the next 24 hours – to plan all that you have to, and want, to do.

Day-Timer
A time-control device manufactured and sold by the Day-Timer company.

Deadline
A date and time by which you need to complete a task.

Delegatee
One who receives assigned tasks.

Delegation
To assign a task to someone else.

Delegator
One who assigns tasks to another.

Expense
An allocated resource, such as money or time, which results in a benefit but no long-term return.

Goal planning
Deciding what you want to have achieved by the last day of your life in each of your seven vital areas. Working backwards to determine what you will have to do each year, each month, each week, and each day to do this.

Gopher
An assistant to help with your errands; often a college student.

Holistic approach
Having all of your to-do items, appointments, and scheduled events in one book or location.

Industrial Revolution
An era that began in England some 200 years ago, when a fundamental shift in economics occurred from agriculture to manufacturing and heralded an age of economic expansion.

Information Age
An era in which ideas rather than physical assets control wealth.

Integration
Having both work and personal calendars in one location to see the "big picture" and how the calendars relate.

Interruption
An unanticipated event that disturbs you either in person or electronically, via telephone, fax, e-mail, beeper, or pager.

Interruptions log
A simple tool you can use to catalog interruptions as they occur, allowing you to take corrective action and prevent repetitive, unimportant interruptions from occurring.

Irritations list
A simple list of things that irritate you. You would take action at times to eliminate some of these irritations.

Investment
Allocating a resource such as money or time and getting a long-term return for the resource spent.

Life-improvement chart
A simple tool you can use to determine where you are now in each of your seven vital areas and where you wish to go in the future.

Meeting
Two or more people getting together to exchange common information.

Multi-tasking
Doing more than one task at a time.

Not crucial
Something that is of low priority.

Organizing your life
The practice of gaining better control, not absolute control, over both your work and home life with simple techniques that free you to focus on the things you consider important.

Paperwork
Information that comes to you in physical form, including mail, e-mails, faxes, and memos.

Pareto Principle
See the 20/80 Rule.

Parkinson's Law
A practical rule that says, in part, that a project tends to take as long as the time allocated for it. If you have one thing to do in a day, it takes all day. If you have two things to do in a day, you generally get both done.

Personal productivity
The measure of all that you accomplish in your work and personal lives, measured against your lifetime goals.

Personal productivity system
A pyramid of building blocks to help you achieve high productivity in your day.

Power of the pen
The act of putting important things into writing so that they are not overlooked.

Prioritizing
Rating tasks in terms of importance, in order to focus your attention on the most important ones.

Prioritizing system
Assigning values to items to be done: A = crucial, B = important, C = of little value, D = of no value, and * = quickie.

Procrastination
Putting off until another day the things you know you ought to be doing today.

Productivity triangle
The three areas of personal self-improvement that will enhance your future success: time management, speed-reading, and communications.

Reverse delegation
Returning a delegated task to the person who delegated it you in the first place.

Scheduled events
A commitment to a certain date and time, whether business or personal. *See also* appointment.

Seven vital areas
The seven important areas that make up our lives: health, family, financial, intellectual, social, professional, and spiritual.

Spring-fever bug
A fictional bug that bites you and lulls you into wasting time. It exists to help you slow down and enjoy your life.

Staff
Employees who report to you.

Sub-prioritizing

Assigning descending values to groups of prioritized tasks. For example, if you have three A tasks, you would sub-prioritize them as A-1, A-2, and A-3, in descending order of their value to you.

Success

When a person identifies their goals and achieves them.

Stress

The effects you feel when circumstances fall short of your expectations.

Stuff

The ongoing flow of little tasks that may occupy your day.

The 20/80 rule

Formally known as the Pareto Principle, it states that 80 percent of business comes from 20 percent of customers.

The 7 x 7 technique

The act of building in one small improvement in each of your seven vital areas to do for the next day, giving yourself the benefit of nearly 2,500 little improvements in your future, by investing only 10 minutes per day.

Time

Your most precious resource. There are 24 hours in every day, seven days in every week, and 168 hours in total available to you.

Time log

A simple tool you can use to catalog how your time is being spent, allowing you to make adjustments to increase your productivity.

Time management

The art, science, and practice of gaining better control (not absolute control) over the 24 hours in your day to create both personal balance and increased productivity.

To-do list

A written list of what you have to do and what you want to do over the next 24 hours.

Uni- or duo-dimensional

Building your life on one or two of the seven vital areas, which places your success at risk if one area were to collapse.

Virtual assistant

An assistant accessed online who can help you accomplish some of your tasks.

Working smart

The practice of leveraging the limited time you have each day to maximize your results by using simple time-management tools.

Index

A

20/80 rule (or 80/20 rule) 78–9, 226, 260
7 x 7 technique 236, 237, 283–95
acknowledging others 283, 290, 295
action 119, 127, 129, 136, 141, 143, 270, 277, 278, 279, 308
address and telephone directory 115, 122, 123, 124, 127
advice 163, 177, 259, 293
agenda 96, 173, 174, 179, 183–5, 188, 189
alpha state 301, 302, 303
amenities 173, 186, 189
anger 131
anniversary 119–20, 127
anticipation 88, 94–6, 99, 107
appointments 64, 87, 88, 90, 92, 94, 96, 98, 99, 101, 169, 189, 288
appreciating others 289
"ask-because" technique 205
assistant 161, 166–7, 169, 209, 214
attention span 138
audiotapes 45–6
authority 161, 197
availability 90
avoidance tactics *see* procrastination

B

balance wheel, the 39, 54–5
balancing your life 39–55, 85, 146, 160, 310, 311
barriers 101
basic values 305–6, 307, 309, 311
bigger-picture 61, 63, 88, 101, 220, 235, 254
birthdays 119–20, 127, 155
blame 290
boredom 29
brainstorm 188
broadening horizons 45
budget 161, 209, 322
building blocks 50, 101
burnout 146, 163

C

calendars 87–99, 119
cash flow 44
challenge 50
changing jobs 163, 326–8, 331
charity 49, 325
chatting 76, 260, 264
children 43, 53, 97, 151, 165, 285, 319–20
choices 32, 34, 195, 294, 295
Christmas 120, 127, 321–2
colleagues *see* coworkers
comfort zone 45, 186
commitments 81, 85, 87, 97, 99, 249
communication 43, 330
communities 49
commuting 44, 45, 46, 92
compliment 288, 290
concentrating resources 80
contacts 154, 155
context 88, 90–3, 99
control 37, 41, 55, 63, 71, 88, 91, 96, 98, 104, 105, 106, 112, 118, 178, 243, 244, 247, 253, 267, 281, 300, 302, 304, 308
corrective steps 228
correspondence 198
coworkers 165, 209, 240, 241, 242, 261, 263, 264, 266
crisis management 100–13, 244
crisis management log 103, 109–13
cross-purposes 59, 61
crucial and non–crucial tasks 73, 74–85, 131, 195, 234, 267

D

daily improvements 124, 127, 284–95
daily planning 57–71, 83, 96, 101, 107, 108, 129, 136, 177, 179, 221, 299, 300, 310, 312
database 154
daydreaming 301, 302
Day-Timer 64, 65, 117, 119, 120, 122, 124, 126, 127
deadlines 96, 103, 108, 112, 139, 140, 161, 163, 203, 210, 243, 244, 278
dedication 163
delegation 44, 68, 83, 100, 145–57, 156–69, 208, 211, 217, 230, 232, 279, 322
    see also reverse delegation and unconscious delegation
demands 32, 245
disappointment 82
discretionary items 64, 108, 169
distractions 194, 201
divorce 43, 311
duo-dimensional 51

E

education 35, 45, 46, 48, 66, 151, 302, 329–30
effectiveness 62
e-mail 203, 204, 208, 213–5, 217, 240, 255
    blocking e–mails 214
emotion 74–5, 131
empowerment 164
energy 40
excuses 104
exercise 42, 285, 323
expectations 32, 82, 83, 85, 156
expertise 159

F

failure 130, 134, 143, 152
family 40, 41, 43, 50, 51, 52, 66, 83, 90, 165, 166, 221, 274, 276, 285, 287, 288, 303, 304, 306, 308, 309, 311, 317, 318–21, 324, 331
fear 130
filing 198, 208, 211, 212, 246, 325
finances 40, 44, 48, 51, 52, 53, 274, 276, 288, 307, 308, 310
fitness see health
flexibility 63, 244
focus 37, 40, 61, 68, 73, 85, 201, 245, 280, 303, 309
follow-up 185
foreign language 45, 47
friends 47–8, 50, 53, 125, 155, 165, 288, 317, 318–21
frustration 33, 230, 231, 242, 259, 321

G

getting started 142
gift list 115, 119, 127
goals and desires 61, 81, 85, 139, 166, 229, 270, 276, 279, 280, 285, 287, 288, 303, 307, 309, 310, 315
gopher see assistant
Gross National Product 78
guilt 131

H

habit 174
happiness 50
health 40, 42, 51, 52, 53, 274, 275, 276, 277, 285, 288, 304, 306, 308, 311
hired help 168, 169 see also assistant
hobby 47, 48, 66, 116, 167

holidays 321–2
holistic approach 87, 88, 99
home 324–6, 331

I

illness 42
important dates 119–20
impromptu meetings 188
index cards 115, 116–21, 127
Industrial Revolution 31, 149
Information Age 31, 33, 45, 329
information, availability of 30, 32, 177,
    195, 243, 329
inner circle 159, 165, 169
integration 88, 97–8, 99
intellectual life 40, 51, 274, 275, 277,
    288, 304, 307
Internet 60, 324, 326
interruptions 37, 68, 107, 216, 221,
    224, 230, 232, 236, 237, 239–67, 279
managing interruptions 243–51
    repetitive interrupters 266
interruptions log 236, 239, 251
interviews 327–8
in-tray 216, 264
investing time 152
irritations list 115, 118–9, 127

J

job opening notice 167
job see professional life
junk mail 75, 76, 206, 214, 217

K

keeping in touch 318–9
keeping track 126
"knowledge is power" 45, 60

L

lateness 112, 180–3
laziness 130, 143
learning see education
leisure time 30, 33, 228, 318–325, 329
letting go 146, 150, 157
library 60
life improvement chart 236, 237, 269–81
life's seven vital areas 39–55, 66, 150,
    207, 237, 269, 270, 274, 276,
    279, 281, 285, 288, 295, 304, 307,
    308, 310
lists 116–121
    see also gift list, irritations list,
    procrastinations list, to-do-list, and
    wish list
logic 74–5

M

mail 221, 287
    see also junk mail and e–mail
mailing lists 203, 204, 206, 214, 217
maintenance 323, 331
management philosophy 160
management skills 45
marriage 42
master plan 63
maximizing results 57
meeting rooms 186
meetings 64, 68, 87, 96, 99 173–89, 221,
    224, 230, 232, 279
meeting attendance 176–8, 189
maximizing meeting time 170, 171,
    173–89
meeting preparation 179
    unnecessary meetings 174–8, 189
memos 204, 217
micro-management 153

money management 35, 51
month-at-a-glance calendar 88, 99
morning people 93
motivation 85, 129, 132, 134, 139, 143, 270, 281

N

natural strengths 93
necessary evils 178
networking 145, 154, 157, 326
New Year's Resolution 139, 278
news 60, 301, 302
night people 93

O

office supplies 117, 122, 124
ordering tasks 81
organizational tools and techniques 39, 64–6, 71, 100, 105, 106, 115–27, 200, 219–35, 270, 281, 317
organizing yourself 27, 39, 115–27, 191–203, 235, 279, 317–31
out of sight, out of mind 192, 201, 212, 324–5
over indulgence 322
over planning 69, 71, 83
overcoming procrastination 129
overcommitment 90, 161, 162
overwhelmed 191, 195, 201

P

pain see pleasure
Palm Pilots 66, 122
paperwork 161, 170, 171, 192, 197, 199, 200, 203–17, 246
    household paperwork 325
Pareto Principal 78, 226, 260

Parkinson's Law 68–9, 83
partner 43, 95, 125, 165, 285, 288, 320
perfectionism 79, 80, 109, 311
personal improvement 329–30, 331
personal life 317–31, 329
personal organizer 65, 66
personal productivity system 236, 237, 297–315
personal time 75, 136, 138
personal wealth 149
personal well-being 323–4
plan ahead 39, 95, 96, 120, 124, 138, 259, 260, 279, 321–2
pleasure and pain 132–3, 134, 195, 201
portable file cabinet 126, 127
positive thinking 301, 303, 304
pressure 39, 50, 55, 69, 71, 75, 79, 104, 193, 228
prevention 105, 109, 112
pride 150
priorities 44, 73–85, 87, 182, 189, 239, 245–7, 251, 267, 299
prioritizing system 73, 75, 80–5, 245–7
problem solving 109
procrastination 100, 101, 129–43, 278
procrastinations list 143
productivity 25, 27, 29 31–7, 41, 59, 61, 62, 71, 77, 81, 82, 93, 95, 109, 113, 123, 125, 131, 136, 150, 171, 193, 198, 199, 200, 203, 220, 228, 229, 231, 234, 235, 241, 242, 252, 283, 299, 312, 324 , 331
    maximizing productivity 248
profession 45, 125
professional life 40, 48, 51, 136, 191, 274, 276, 288, 307, 310, 329
purpose 58

Q

quality versus quantity 75
questioning 164

R

rating performance 52, 54–5
rating productivity 36
rationalize 92
rat-race 33, 59
reading 53, 66
  inspirational reading 303, 304, 306
speed-reading 46, 330
realistic aims 77, 79
relationships 35, 49, 83, 307, 321
religion 49 see also spiritual life
renegotiating 163
resistance levels 40
resources 57, 60, 299
responsibilities 25, 32, 34, 81, 85,
  162, 266, 310, 321
restaurant 186
resumé 327–8
reverse delegation 159, 161, 162–4, 169
rewards 31, 50, 311
risk of collapse 51
role models 313–4

S

satisfaction 48, 69, 85, 134, 270,
  283, 331
saying "no" 248
scheduled event 64, 87–99, 101,
  169, 189
scheduling 43, 47, 48, 139, 191,
  197, 201, 211, 212, 217, 279, 281,
  321, 331
screening paperwork 203, 208–9, 217

self-screening 209
seminars 45
sense of importance 146
shopping 166, 322, 326
skills 35, 45
sleep 40, 58, 83, 300–1, 312, 322,
  323–4
social life 40, 41, 47, 51, 191, 274,
  288, 304, 307
spiritual life 40, 41, 49, 51, 274,
  275, 288, 308
spontaneity 63
sport 42, 48
spouse see partner
stability 40
staff 37, 159, 160–1, 169, 208, 209, 217
state of mind 135, 143
step-by-step approach 138, 315
stress 25, 32, 33, 37, 75, 82–3, 95, 96,
  104, 113, 118, 131, 134, 138, 163,
  199, 230, 242, 259, 300–1, 304, 311,
  312, 321, 322, 329
stress reduction 73, 82–3, 85
success 31, 41, 50, 73, 101, 108, 125,
  131, 138, 157, 229, 297, 299, 331
short-term success 51, 306, 311, 315
steps for success 299–315
surprises 290
survival instinct 132

T

targets 278
technology 30
telephone calls 139, 181–2, 221, 240,
  241, 242, 255, 259, 318
telephone directory see address
thanking others 289
tidy desk 161, 191–201, 309
time budget 39, 51, 52, 55

time limits 80
time log 170, 171, 219–35
time management 25–37, 68, 73, 74,
    90, 96, 101, 104, 105, 106, 113,
    146, 161, 174, 214, 220, 229, 231,
    269, 279, 309, 310, 329
time off 75, 232, 249
time saving 208, 209
time wasting 68, 174–89, 229, 234, 262–3,
    279
timekeeping 180–3
to-do list 41, 57, 61, 64–71, 73, 74, 82,
    84–5, 87, 101, 108, 138, 169, 197,
    198, 199, 201, 212, 217, 240, 242,
    245, 246, 247, 249, 259, 270, 278,
    279, 285, 287, 308, 309, 310, 319
trash 198
travel 123–4

U

unconscious delegation 147
uni–dimensional 51
unpleasant tasks 139
urgency 68

V

vacation 94–6
virtual assistants 167
voice mail 204, 217
voluntary work 48, 49

W

waking up 301–3, 312
walking 303–4, 324
wallet 126, 127
wealth 33
weekend getaways 320

"what goes around comes around" 289,
    291, 294
wind down 301
wish list 117
work area 170, 171, 191–201, 309,
    324–5
work ethic 34, 59
work experience 209
work levels 31, 44, 59, 163
work load 161
working hours 30, 44
working smart 34, 230, 279, 329
working together 59–60
workshops 45

Y

year-round planning 120

Acknowledgments

Author's Acknowledgments

Any worthwhile endeavor is the result of several talented people working together and three unique professionals who have worked on this project with me deserve high praise and recognition for their efforts. First, my thanks and gratitude to my literary agent, John Willig, a true professional, who initiated this project and provided the needed encouragement all along the way to final completion. Second, to Lynn Northrup, my thanks and gratitude to a terrific editor who was able to take my initial manuscripts and shape and polish them into a shining text that will help to make a difference in a lot of people's lives. And, third, to Jennifer Williams, my thanks and gratitude to a one-of-a-kind managing editor who thoughtfully prepared me for every step along the way to completing this book and supervised the process step-by-step to a successful completion with her compassionate coaching and always helpful suggestions.

Publisher's Acknowledgments

Dorling Kindersley would like to thank Neal Cobourne for jacket design and Beth Apple for jacket text.

Picture Credits

The publisher would like to thank the following for their kind permission to reproduce their photographs: (Abbreviations key t=top, b=bottom, r=right, l=left)

Comstock: 32 (t), 34, 35, 53 (t), 74, 75, 77, 81, 93 (t), 105, 108, 110, 131, 132, 135, 140, 146, 154, 207, 211, 212, 215, 329. **Greg Evans International Photo Library:** 24, 25, 29, 30, 36 (t), 37, 38, 41, 43, 44 (t), 49, 51 (t, b), 55, 67, 71, 72, 85, 100, 101, 118, 125, 130, 133, 136, 139, 151, 153, 156, 157, 160, 166, 169, 174, 176, 179, 181, 187, 193, 200, 204, 206, 217, 218, 220, 221, 224, 225, 229, 230, 233, 234, 236, 237, 241, 244, 246, 247, 249, 250, 251, 255, 256, 261, 265, 272, 274, 276, 277, 278, 281, 289, 295, 296, 299, 304, 309, 310, 311 (b), 313, 321, 322, 331. **PhotoDisc:** 28, 31 (t, b), 32 (b), 33, 36 (b), 44 (b), 46, 47 (t, b), 48, 56, 60, 61, 63, 64, 65 (b), 66, 68, 69, 76 (b), 80, 82, 83 (t, b), 91, 95, 98, 106, 107, 111, 123, 124, 141, 149, 150, 162, 175, 180, 183, 194, 216, 268. **Robert Harding Picture Library:** 86, 128, 168, 188, 189, 199, 202, 214, 228, 245, 252, 254, 282, 303, 308, 316, 318, 323. **Topham Picturepoint:** 58, 59, 62, 65 (t), 76 (t), 92, 97, 99, 102, 104, 109, 112, 113, 114, 119, 121, 134, 144, 158, 165, 170, 171, 172, 178, 205, 210, 226, 238, 240, 243, 259, 260, 262, 267, 275, 279, 284, 285, 286, 287, 290, 291, 293, 294, 300, 301, 302, 305, 306, 307, 312, 314 (t, b), 315, 319, 320, 324, 325, 326, 327, 328.

Jacket picture credits

Front jacket: Topham Picturepoint
Back jacket: Comstock tl; PhotoDisc ml
Jacket photograph reproduced courtesy of **Palm TM Handheld Computers.**

All other images © Dorling Kindersley.
For further information see: www.dkimages.com